...In All
Our Affairs

Making Crises
Work for You

...In All Our Affairs

Making Crises Work for You

The Al-Anon Family Groups are a fellowship of relatives and friends of alcoholics who share their experience, strength, and hope in order to solve their common problems. We believe alcoholism is a family illness and that changed attitudes can aid recovery.

Al-Anon is not allied with any sect, denomination, political entity, organization, or institution; does not engage in any controversy; neither endorses nor opposes any cause. There are no dues for membership. Al-Anon is self-supporting through its own voluntary contributions.

Al-Anon has but one purpose: to help families of alcoholics. We do this by practicing the Twelve Steps, by welcoming and giving comfort to families of alcoholics, and by giving understanding and encouragement to the alcoholic.

Suggested Preamble to the Twelve Steps

For information and a catalog of literature write:
Al-Anon Family Group Headquarters, Inc.
1600 Corporate Landing Parkway
Virginia Beach, Virginia 23454-5617
Phone: 757-563-1600 Fax: 757-563-1655
www.al-anon.alateen.org/members
e-mail: wso@al-anon.org

Al-Anon/Alateen is supported by members' voluntary contributions and from the sale of our Conference Approved Literature.

This book is also available in: Finnish, French, Italian, and Spanish.

Library of Congress Catalog Card No. 90-84512

©AL-ANON FAMILY GROUP HEADQUARTERS, INC. 1990, 2005
ISBN-978-9-910034-73-9

Approved by
World Service Conference
Al-Anon Family Groups

Al-Anon books that may be helpful:

Alateen—Hope for Children of Alcoholics (B-3)

The Dilemma of the Alcoholic Marriage (B-4)

The Al-Anon Family Groups—Classic Edition (B-5)

One Day at a Time in Al-Anon (B-6), Large Print (B-14)

Lois Remembers (B-7)

Al-Anon's Twelve Steps & Twelve Traditions (B-8)

Alateen—a day at a time (B-10)

As We Understood... (B-11)

Courage to Change—One Day at a Time in Al-Anon II (B-16), Large Print (B-17)

From Survival to Recovery: Growing Up in an Alcoholic Home (B-21)

How Al-Anon Works for Families & Friends of Alcoholics (B-22)

Courage to Be Me—Living with Alcoholism (B-23)

Paths to Recovery—Al-Anon's Steps, Traditions, and Concepts (B-24)

Living Today in Alateen (B-26)

Hope for Today (B-27), Large Print (B-28)

CONTENTS

PREFACE

Life presents us with many difficult situations that can be overwhelming unless we are able to respond effectively. Those whose lives have been affected by the family disease of alcoholism are acutely aware of such crises, whether they result directly from alcoholism or have been worsened by it. This book presents the experiences of many individuals who have used the powerful tools of Al-Anon to deal with some of the difficult situations that confronted them. Our remarkable program of recovery through the Twelve Steps led them to realize that there is no situation too difficult to be bettered and no unhappiness too great to be lessened. By applying the Al-Anon ideas, they found it was possible for them to gain a new perspective on their problems, one that often led to solutions. In effect, they were able to make their crises work for them.

The emphasis in these stories is not on the problem but on the use of the Al-Anon program to alleviate it. They represent a wide variety of situations and lifestyles, none of which should be regarded as reflecting either approval or disapproval. The words and circumstances are those of the person sharing; the actual actions they have taken are also their own and are not recommended as universally applicable solutions.

Nor does their arrangement imply any ranking or

rating of the difficulty of any given situation. For each of us, our own situation is the most difficult because it is the one through which we are struggling. The true importance of these shared experiences lies in how Al-Anon helped each person arrive at a means of dealing with their particular problem. Whatever the individual circumstances, we can all gain courage and strength from others' success stories. As these stories so clearly demonstrate, by following the Al-Anon path to recovery, we too may have a spiritual awakening and come to "practice these principles in all our affairs."

INTRODUCTION

Alcoholism is an enormously powerful family disease. Even in the best of times, we who have experienced the effects of this disease may struggle to maintain a sense of balance in our lives. Sometimes, just when we think we can't handle one more problem, a new crisis leads us to feel trapped in an endless tunnel of suffering. Longtime members as well as newcomers can face infidelity, illness, violence, divorce, death, incest, and a host of other very trying situations. The Al-Anon program offers us the support, as well as the tools, to acknowledge, accept, and deal with these problems in a safe and loving atmosphere.

In the past, we may have tried reaching out for help to friends or family members who did not understand the family disease of alcoholism. These exchanges left many of us feeling guilty, ashamed, and determined to keep our troubles to ourselves. In a world where the admission of a problem is often mistaken for weakness and where furtive silence is confused with loyalty, it was hard to believe that opening up to others would yield anything but embarrassment and pain. We felt more alone than ever.

But we are not alone. No matter what the difficulty, no matter how unique we may feel, somewhere nearby are men and women with similar stories who have found help, comfort, and hope through recovery in Al-Anon. In meetings, over coffee, on the telephone, in Al-Anon literature, and through sponsorship, we discover that other members of the fellowship have felt what we feel. In time we feel safe enough to let out the dark secrets.

Many who have come through periods of turmoil with the help of the Al-Anon program recall that gradually, almost without our knowing it, our lives began to change. The healing love we received when we reached out for help in Al-Anon helped us to love ourselves. Al-Anon's Twelve Steps offered a concrete strategy for dealing with the situation realistically. We came to believe that, although we may be powerless over our circumstances, there is a Power greater than ourselves who is not. We didn't necessarily get the results we wanted, but somehow we always seemed to get what we needed. We began to find some peace, to take life more lightly, and to remember how to laugh. The "hopeless" situation stopped looking so bleak. Ironically, the crisis often inspired long-needed changes in our attitudes and habits, opening doors that allowed joy to enter. How astonishing that our greatest tragedy could lead to important personal growth and healing.

So we offer some thoughts about this miraculous process, drawn from Al-Anon members from all over the world. Their backgrounds are as varied as the problems they have faced. They do not offer advice, nor claim that every obstacle can be happily overcome. Instead they share personal experiences that have marked their journey from suffering to serenity.

A Special Word to Anyone Confronted with Violence

Al-Anon's gentle process unfolds gradually, over time. But those of us facing violent, potentially life-threatening situations may have to make immediate choices to ensure safety for ourselves and our children. This may mean arranging for a safe house with a neighbor or friend, calling for police protection, or leaving money and an extra set of car keys where they can be collected at any time in case of emergency.

It is not necessary to decide how to resolve the situation once and for all—only how to get out of harm's way until this process of awareness, acceptance, and action can free us to make choices for ourselves that we can live with.

Anyone who has been physically or sexually abused or even threatened may be terrified of taking action at all. It can require every ounce of courage and faith to act decisively. But no one has to accept violence. No matter what seems to trigger the attack, we all deserve to be safe.

Tapping Other Resources

Al-Anon's purpose is to help families and friends of alcoholics. We come together to find help and support in dealing with the effects of alcoholism. In time we discover that the principles of our program can be practiced "in all our affairs." But there are times when, in order to work through especially challenging circumstances, we may need more specialized support from mental, spiritual, physical, or legal advisors. Many of us

have benefited from taking care of these needs in addition to coming to Al-Anon.

Part One

Awareness

CHAPTER ONE

Becoming Aware

It is said that we never get more than we can handle. This can be hard to believe as we watch the door slam shut on several years of marriage or sit in an emergency room with undeniably broken bones from the latest violent alcoholic episode. Sometimes we face up to a difficult situation at the first sign of trouble, but often we, who have been affected by someone else's drinking, try to pretend that the problem doesn't exist, or hope that it will go away. We may isolate ourselves, fearing other people's reactions. Or we avoid talking about it, believing that the situation will become more real if we name it out loud. We might want to be aware, to know exactly what is going on, but we also want to avoid more bad news. This is a form of denial. When we are in denial we perceive a situation to be so threatening that we adapt by denying it exists in order to survive. We make the best choice we can according to the world we see. Sometimes only a crisis can break through our denial. As the situation worsens, facing the truth often becomes the better choice.

At other times, awareness comes to us slowly and gently, and we have the luxury of relinquishing denial little by little, replacing it with the sense of security that

frequently develops in Al-Anon, regardless of our problems. Identifying with other members as they face their
own truths, seeing the courage all around us, and being
totally free from pressure to do it "the right way" encourages us to feel safe. As that feeling grows, long-buried
awareness can begin to awaken within us.

For some, memories of an alcoholic's verbal or physical abuse suddenly erupt into consciousness after being
lost for many years. We may not welcome these memories; we may even actively resist them. Awareness can
be very upsetting when it shatters our old ideas about
ourselves and others.

Beginners are not the only ones who have difficulty
coping with trying situations. Even longtime members,
accustomed to relatively serene lives, may be reluctant
to acknowledge the strain of a crisis. It's easy to delude
ourselves that, with enough recovery, nothing should
bother us. On the contrary, as we recover, we begin to
feel all our feelings and participate in life more fully.
We often gain new insights and see things from other
perspectives. When the focus has truly been taken off
the alcoholic and we experience spiritual growth in
Al-Anon, many of us begin to learn for the first time
who we are and what we want. While this process often
allows us to discover previously unrecognized assets
and talents that greatly enhance our lives, we may also
uncover areas of discontent. Some become aware of
deep dissatisfaction with careers or finances. Others
question moral choices. An honest appraisal of personal
truth may allow a middle-aged father to accept that he

might be gay. It may encourage a homemaker to apply to medical school or tempt an attorney to leave a lucrative practice to write poetry. It is traumatic, to say the least, to be faced with such major discoveries.

Awareness can also be thrust upon us with staggering abruptness. Who wouldn't feel devastated by a loved one's suicide? Who wouldn't be gripped with fear upon discovering a lump in a breast or learning that a former lover may have exposed us to a potentially fatal disease? How many can respond gracefully when the process of aging makes once-simple tasks impossible to perform? The family disease of alcoholism can leave us feeling completely overwhelmed by such situations. We may have no control over our circumstances, and we may feel abandoned by those from whom we most crave support. But we do have choices. We can decide whether or not we will abandon ourselves. One way to honor ourselves is to allow the truth as we perceive it to surface, in its own way and at its own pace.

Reflections on Becoming Aware

Facing Reality

As the child of alcoholic parents, I learned at a young age that appearances were all-important. We were considered a model family and took great pains to keep it that way. But the picture-perfect image we showed to others had nothing to do with the way things really were. Life in my house wasn't very pretty—there were brutal beatings, vicious verbal assaults, threats, and intimidation. This reality was never discussed. Not only were we fooling others, we were also fooling ourselves. Denial was our lifestyle.

I remained in denial, even as an adult, until I found myself homeless when an alcoholic relationship ended. I had heard about Al-Anon before, but it took a desperate situation to get me there. I had nowhere else to go. My family had refused to help in any way, and I had no savings. I felt guilty, because I had known that this could happen and in my denial, had done nothing to prepare. I blamed everyone I could think of, but bitterness wasn't putting a roof over my head.

I shared briefly at my very first Al-Anon meeting, saying only that my alcoholic girlfriend had thrown me out. I was so embarrassed, so ashamed of what other people would think! I couldn't bring myself to mention that I was now sleeping in my car. Even so, I was relieved to finally be telling a bit of the truth. I never expected anyone to understand, much less care about me, but people at the meeting were incredibly kind and supportive, so I kept coming back.

It has been a long, slow process to come face to face with a lifetime of denial. The shame that I learned in my alcoholic home made this difficult. I discovered a part of myself that felt so flawed and unworthy that I thought I deserved to live on the street. As I listened and identified with others in Al-Anon meetings, it became easier to admit the truth about my circumstances and my feelings. I learned that my situation had the effects of alcoholism written all over it. In time I was able to talk about living in my car, and when members of the fellowship offered assistance, I was able to accept it. Eventually I saved enough money to get a place of my own.

A wonderful Sponsor has helped me immeasurably. He encouraged me to "let time take time," and guided me through the Steps. With his help I have begun to question my attitudes about myself and take a closer and less fearful look at my past. Through this process I have come to believe in a Power greater than myself. I am learning to trust that He or She will guide me to what is best for me. I cling to the slogans when the pain is great, repeating "Let Go and Let God," "Easy Does It," and "Keep It Simple" again and again. Sometime I even find comfort by repeating the Suggested Al-Anon/Alateen Welcome to myself between meetings. The disease of alcoholism is so much bigger than I am, and I have to practice remembering that I am powerless over it. Today

I feel so lucky, because I know that my Higher Power is even greater than alcoholism.

Coming to See Reality

I am one of the many who felt wrong from the very beginning of my life, born female when a male was desired by my alcoholic parent. I was also a dreamer. I escaped into my fantasy land where no one could hurt me, my parents loved me greatly, and the world was mine. But it was a lonely existence. I thought that if only I could die, I wouldn't have to put up with all that was happening in my life.

As an adult, my home was full of the family disease of alcoholism. The worst symptom was the abuse—physical, mental, and spiritual. Some of us gave this abuse, others suffered from it, and still others received it from one person and gave it to another. At one point, I made plans to attend an Al-Anon meeting. As I stood outside the door, I heard the Twelve Steps being read. Then someone else arrived, and I left, gripped with fear. Two years later, after more violence at home, I finally made it inside the room.

Slowly I have come to see reality. It is hard to look at me—the imperfect me—and even harder to work on me. But I am beginning to know the difference between fantasy and reality. Though I once thought I was wronged in my life, I know now that I wronged myself. I took my own rights away from me.

My first two years of Al-Anon were spent sorting, looking, absorbing, and germinating. I began to feel that

I could cope. Maybe I could be the wife and mother I wanted to be, even though my husband was still drinking actively. I had taken the first three Steps. I admitted I was powerless. I could see that my life had become unmanageable. I knew only my Higher Power could restore me to sanity, and I turned over my will and my life. I was beginning to understand that I had to open the door to Him. His door was already open to me.

Awakening from the Nightmare

Before I found Al-Anon, our home life was constantly disrupted by rows. Our eldest son was living away from home, having been "asked" to leave once again by my alcoholic husband.

Early one morning our house was surrounded by police. They were looking for my son, as there had been an attempted robbery at his previous place of employment by somebody answering his description. My son had been fired the previous week. I laughed shakily, "It won't be my son, he's far too sensible to do anything that silly." Twenty-four hours later, after he was arrested, he admitted to armed robbery. One evening while awaiting the trial, I saw him being slapped repeatedly by my husband. I was pleading with my husband to stop, and our youngest was crying in the bedroom. Why was this nightmare happening? I had heard of Al-Anon, and right then and there I decided to attend meetings. What a relief it was to find people who understood.

I felt terrible remorse at seeing my darling, mixed-up son condemned to three years hard labor. How I wished

I had been more aware of his disturbed emotional state, that I had done things differently. If only I had come to Al-Anon earlier. Eventually I learned to let go of past regrets and to be grateful for the understanding I achieved after I did reach Al-Anon. With God's help I won't repeat past mistakes. We have been blessed with another son, who is now learning that Daddy is sick but still loves him dearly.

Our eldest son was paroled after 18 months. Miraculously, he's started a new life, has a job, and is engaged to a nice girl. We have a better relationship now, as I "Let Go and Let God." I can't imagine where I would be today without the help of Al-Anon.

Changing a Pattern of Denial

During my teenage years, my sisters and I were molested by one of my father's employees. When we told my mother about these incidents, she was shocked and angry. We thought she would take care of the situation. Within a few weeks, however, we realized that our parents were not dealing with this child molester. We were left to fend for ourselves.

My husband did not drink when I married him, but when he did start drinking the disease progressed rapidly. Although my husband did not physically abuse the children and me, we were emotionally and verbally abused. At age four, my son was very withdrawn and fearful, and my two-year-old daughter would not approach her father. All my fears from youth returned and I became immobilized. Through the grace of God

I found Al-Anon. It took more than two years in the program before it occurred to me that I had become like my mother. I was not accepting the responsibility of protecting my children from emotional and verbal abuse. I prayed for wisdom, guidance, and the courage to change the things I could. With the help of my Higher Power and some special Al-Anon friends, I gained the courage to leave my husband for a while. It was a difficult, painful, and lonely time, but Al-Anon helped me through it.

Since then my husband has achieved sobriety in AA. The children are no longer afraid of him. We are trying to grow as individuals, in a family built on love, acceptance, and trust.

Facing a Painful Past

When I was 19 years old, I started dating. I wanted a man to love me and get me out of my parents' home. When I became pregnant, I was ashamed and very afraid. I was positive I was pregnant, but my alcoholic boyfriend convinced me I wasn't. I started taking the birth control pill. I don't know how many pills I took.

Soon after that, I had a miscarriage. I was horrified! When my boyfriend finally arrived, he was too drunk to realize what I was talking about. I thought I was responsible because I had taken those pills, and I felt like a murderer. Today I know this is impossible—the pills could not have been the cause. At the time, however, I didn't know any better. I had no one to talk to about it.

My boyfriend became my husband. I felt I had to

marry him because I had killed his baby.

Al-Anon helped me to look at my miscarriage objectively. I told members of the fellowship what had happened, and they understood and loved me anyway. Then one night I had a flashback. My mind took me back through the horror of that night when I was 19 years old. I have heard in meetings that if we don't face something when it is happening, we will have to face it later in order to deal with it. When I went through my miscarriage again, I called a friend in Al-Anon and she loved me through it. I saw the blood. I felt the fear. I experienced the pain. I then realized that I can forgive myself for something I did so many years ago. I can forgive that young girl who was so frightened.

Breaking the Isolation

I wish there were more men in the program. I sometimes feel like an ambassador for my gender, and I feel uncomfortable with that role.

I know several men in the fellowship who grew up with alcoholism, as I did. They have helped me understand and accept the isolation that I lived with and even cultivated. Feeling closer to these people, I have come to feel closer to myself. Hearing the struggles these men have had establishing intimacy in their lives and making room for their feelings, I have been able to be gentler and more understanding with myself. The presence of men in Al-Anon has helped remind me that alcoholism affects us all without regard to gender or background. The gift of serenity is available to everyone.

Overcoming Denial

Anger, bitterness, fear, rejection, and inadequacy were the feelings I fought so hard to deny throughout the 26 years of my marriage to an active alcoholic who had numerous affairs. Delusion became my way of life. I forced myself to see him as I wanted him to be, not as he really was, and to maintain the appearance of the "cute little couple" we were so often called. I convinced myself I could live without feeling anything, the only way I knew to stop the pain.

It took many months of Al-Anon meetings before I felt enough trust to share about this. I first needed to believe that my husband's behavior was not a reflection on me. The Serenity Prayer was a great source of comfort and guidance. I hated the past and wanted desperately to change it.

I have made peace with the past by realizing I cannot cure the problems my husband has that caused him to make these choices. When I long to change my husband, I can remember the Al-Anon slogan, "Let It Begin with Me," and turn my attention to my own attitudes. When old feelings haunt me, I quickly make a gratitude list. I find this a great way to banish ugly thoughts and feelings. From many years of misery to three challenging but oh-so-fulfilling years of recovery, I am changing my life with the help of Al-Anon, the program of hope!

Listening to Inner Awareness

I found out that my alcoholic husband had molested a young girl only when the case came to court. At first

I was angry, hurt, and in shock. But the biggest problem has been my anger at myself because there had been warning signals that I hadn't heeded. I had pushed aside my feelings, thinking they were not worth anything. Through Al-Anon, I am learning to trust that my feelings do have some basis in reality and are worth listening to. I really believe we all have our own answers within ourselves and can find them with the help of our Al-Anon program and a Higher Power.

Living in the Present

I remember the lonely nights, the long waits, wondering who he was with and what he was doing. I remember how my suspicions were aroused as his advances to other women became more publicly aggressive. These fears were somehow tempered by hearing only what I wanted to hear and by believing because I so wanted to believe.

Intent on creating the marriage of my dreams, I chose to set aside all the tell-tale signs of the *today* I was in. I saw them as the hard times I must ride through in order to reach the promise of a better tomorrow.

Alcoholism, the family disease, progressed. The hard times continued to get worse until I found Al-Anon and my attitudes began to change. The Al-Anon program, the people in it, the meetings, and an active Sponsor help to remind me who I am, where I've been, where I am right now, and that I need to be open to whatever may come tomorrow. Security—or my search for it—is no longer my base of operations. I can see that nothing in my life has ever been forever. The good and the bad pass. I no longer have to live in the unreality of a tomorrow I've already scripted but which may never come to pass.

Healing by Sharing

. . . So, tell us about your life just before coming to Al-Anon.

. . . Well, it was truly unmanageable—ugly. I had a lover who was drinking and drugging; he was also in denial that I had the AIDS virus. And I was not exactly handling my AIDS diagnosis in a healthy, positive way.

. . . What did you hope to get from Al-Anon?

. . . Actually, I just wanted to get the strength to leave my lover—and as soon as possible. It was quite a shock when I heard the suggestion not to make any radical changes in my life for six months!!!

. . . So what did you do?

. . . I hung in there, one day at a time, and then a miracle happened. My lover hit a bottom, and although I only had a few meetings behind me, they were enough to prevent me from reacting to him the way I had in the past. He started a Twelve Step program three days later and stuck with it. Then we hardly saw one another and when we did we were invariably at home making program calls. But our love was strong enough. We realized we were both making dramatic, positive, healing changes in our lives, and these changes, although frightening and sometimes painful, could give our relationship new and exciting dimensions. Today we have a much more honest, trusting, loving relationship.

. . . So you're grateful for what you've learned in Al-Anon?

. . . In more ways than I can say. When I joined Al-Anon, I never thought for one minute that it could possibly affect how I felt about living with the AIDS virus. But when I apply the program to all aspects of my life, miracles can happen. In Al-Anon I've learned that I have choices in my life. These choices apply beautifully to surviving and thriving with the AIDS virus. It took a while for me to pluck up the courage to share about my health status. I had to know that I was in a safe environment. Once I had shared, amazing inner healing began, and I had an incredible outpouring of love and support, even though not everyone is comfortable hearing about it. I choose not to dwell too much on the doom and gloom side of AIDS, but more on the joy of being alive and appreciating the gifts I have. Today I am the happiest person I have ever been—and just for today, that is enough.

Awareness and Shame

My dreams for my children were shattered the day my daughter said, "Mom, I have something to tell you that you aren't going to want to hear." Then she told me about being sexually abused by her brother. My shame was enormous. I am a religious professional and a counselor, and these things weren't supposed to happen in my family. Somehow the Higher Power I had come to know in Al-Anon, the One who cared, came through for me at this time. I knew we had been given this burden and we were strong enough to handle it. I got on the phone immediately and began contacting my Al-Anon support system. I felt suicidal and homicidal. After all the time and energy spent recovering from alcoholism's impact on the family, this new trial just didn't seem fair. I railed against God about the injustices of life. Yet I was frequently moved to tears by the non-judgmental acceptance and support I received.

Within 11 days our son was out of the house. The decision to press charges was made—he was in total denial of his actions. The whole family began to receive counseling. Also some touching, beginning moments of healing were experienced by our daughter, and our son entered a psychiatric hospital. My Al-Anon friends carried me through these early, agonizing days and beyond.

Our son has been diagnosed as having brain damage. Finding appropriate help for him is arduous and exhausting. He falls through the cracks of so many systems, and not everyone is willing to accept a child molester. My daughter dips in and out of depression and is currently having difficulty in school. Al-Anon members love me and remind me of the courage it takes to handle a situation like this with dignity and maturity. With their help, I have been able to deal with teachers without being overcome with shame.

Doing a Fourth and Fifth Step on all this has been extremely painful. I continue to struggle with my shame. I question what is enabling and what is accepting the things I cannot change. There are no easy answers, but my Higher Power has sent others to me with similar experiences to help me apply the principles. With the help of the Al-Anon program, I am coming to accept life on life's terms and find some serenity in the midst of the pain.

Facing My Own Unacceptable Behavior

Through Al-Anon I have recently become aware of how abusive I have been as a result of living in an alcoholic situation. In my own fears, as well as insecurities and frustrations at not being able to control the alcoholic, I have lashed out verbally at my children in name-calling, in irrational hysterics over something as simple as a spilled glass of milk, or in rigid demands for "perfect performance." This awareness has helped me to learn not to react in anger, to stop and think, and to live my life one minute at a time if necessary. Al-Anon has helped me work toward a calmer and more serene life, with more respect for myself and for others.

Letting Go of Denial

By the end of my first year in Al-Anon, I felt a peace I'd never experienced before. When my brother was killed while driving drunk, however, Al-Anon became my lifeline. I discovered I had developed a deep faith that, when tested, remained as solid as a rock. During this time I came to really believe that alcoholism was a disease. I was able to forgive my brother for the slip that caused his death after five years in AA. I learned the meaning of "powerlessness" and "acceptance."

I had learned in Al-Anon to look for opportunities for growth in every situation. This attitude allowed me to gain many spiritual riches from the pain I was experiencing. Only I had the power to turn my pain to gain.

Six months later I was able to admit for the first time that my father was an alcoholic. In admitting this fact, I felt I was betraying my family. I discovered first-hand what a strong hold denial had over me and how it kept me from growing. I am grateful that the merry-go-round has stopped and that I have gotten off in time.

Abandoning Perfectionism

Somewhere in my life I had accepted the idea that I must be perfect or I was nothing. I spent all my time trying to be the perfect wife, mother, daughter, and student. I felt that the only thing keeping me from being perfect was the alcoholic in my life, who shamed me by sleeping with other women and by forcing me to assume all financial responsibility for the family. As time went on I accused him of having an affair with every female he knew. I made a bigger fool of myself than he ever could have done. I filed for a divorce in a smug, self-righteous way, but after he was gone, I came to the bitter realization that I still was not perfect. The awareness was shattering. I felt all alone, angry at the entire world, and that it would be better if I were dead. Fortunately, some very wise Al-Anon members sensed the depths of my despair. They called me when I couldn't call them. They let me cry on their shoulders, and when I told them my deepest secrets they didn't shudder, but hugged me instead. It was the people in the program who kept me from going under. I was not able to see how the Steps could help me with my life, but I sensed the hope, and that is what I held on to.

Today I can accept myself for what I am because I know that whatever happens, I have a Higher Power and a group of people who will love me anyway. Today I can let people see me cry. New-found courage and honesty have helped me see the role I played in the break-up of my marriage, and my husband and I are currently living together once again. It is not easy and I don't know what the outcome will be. I do know that if I take it "One Day at a Time" and live the Al-Anon program as best I can, everything will come out the best possible way, which is close enough to perfect for me.

An End to Denial

Denial gradually slipped away during my first year in Al-Anon, but when my alcoholic boyfriend ended our relationship "for the sake of his recovery," all remaining denial went up like a curtain, leaving me deeply shaken. Something inside me knew that facing reality, with all its broken dreams and disappointments, was the only way to heal. Just exactly when I needed it, a longtime member of Al-Anon was put in my life, like an angel. She walked me to meetings and, at a time when every phone call felt like a terrible imposition, constantly urged me to call. She told me how inspiring it was for her to watch me go through this process. At the time, I thought she was just being nice, but now, some years later, having been on the other side, I know she was sincere. It continues to amaze me how much courage surrounds me in Al-Anon. It is a great privilege to be able to share in it on either side.

Progress, not Perfection

At a workshop on the problems of longtime members in Al-Anon, everyone mentioned the unwillingness of newer Al-Anon members to accept that those of us who have been around a while can still hurt. Likewise, some longtime members think they cannot be sick or have any emotional problems—or at least they must not let anyone know it if they are.

I faced this particular obstacle some years back when I had a paralyzing depression. I was afraid that if less experienced Al-Anon members knew about it, they would think Al-Anon didn't work or that I was some kind of failure. I know now that the Al-Anon fellowship is in the hands of God, not of any person, and that you only expect progress from me, not perfection.

Sometimes I think I hurt more now than I did in the early days, because the more I am aware, the more I feel. Of course I have tools now to help me handle the pain. I don't suffer as long and I don't suffer alone. Still, I feel like saying sometimes, "Tell me again how happy I am."

The longer I am in the program, the harder it is to find people who are where I am in my spiritual journey. To me, this is not snobbery—oh, how guilty I had been feeling about this!—but only fact. Nevertheless, when I get in a rut in Al-Anon, I try to remember that a rut is a grave with both ends knocked out. I can climb out if I don't want to be buried.

Replacing Fantasies with Self-Worth

Today I recognize that in the past I had chosen people I thought I could control, care for, and fix. I unknowingly chose people who would emotionally abuse me to confirm my poor self-esteem, and reject me so I could feel sorry for myself (poor me, I always get hurt). If someone tried to get too close, I shut down. I turned cold. I was afraid of getting too close or being loved because deep inside I didn't feel worthy. I lived in a world of fantasy, always wishing, dreaming, and hoping for what I myself could not give or accept.

In Al-Anon I am learning about me and how to own and change my behavior. As I do, I feel better about myself. Today, as a result of going to meetings and being willing to be honest, I have some self-worth, and don't need to live in fantasy. My life gets better when I take responsibility for just me. Today I will mind my own business and keep my focus where it belongs—on me.

Ending My Isolation

When my alcoholic husband left, it was as if someone had pulled a cord and I didn't have anything or anyone left—not even myself. I was in trouble, totally frightened, and alone. I was a victim with no choices, going nowhere fast. I crawled into Al-Anon.

One of the first things I heard was that it was okay to come any way I was. Many mornings I could barely get up. It was okay if I just attended the meeting and sat there crying. It didn't matter if I was a mess. Meetings broke my isolation. I got phone numbers and realized that the choice was mine whether or not to be alone.

Recovery in Al-Anon required continually making decisions. I had lots of choices and I hadn't been taking responsibility for them. Things didn't just happen to me; I let them happen by not being an active participant. But I didn't have to do anything until I felt ready.

Today I have some clarity. If I didn't have Al-Anon, I'd still be wishing things were different. Longtime Al-Anon members talk about "Live and Let Live." To me this means that the way to a serene life is to live my life to the fullest and let other people live theirs.

Recognizing a Destructive Situation

I know I was fearful of rocking the boat of a potentially suicidal husband, but there was also a lot of denial on my part about how urgent and destructive the situation was. I had tolerated his abusive treatment of the children for a long time. I was pretty casual about my Al-Anon meetings, attending only once a week. My son would come to me saying that Dad had hit him with a shovel. My husband would say he had barely tapped him. I was so confused I could not put "First Things First." I got as upset over my husband growing a beard as I did about his screaming at the children. In time, the things I heard in Al-Anon began to sink in, and my denial broke down. I began to see how destructive the family situation had become, and I made a serious commitment to working the Al-Anon program. I went to a great many meetings, got a Sponsor, and worked the Steps. The slogans helped me so much! They were simple enough to grab onto, even in the midst of my confusion.

Things are so much better today, and I am grateful for what Al-Anon did. However, I wish I had chosen a total immersion in the Al-Anon program right from the beginning. My children are doing well, but I can see the scars. I still have work to do on forgiving myself. I know I did the best I could at the time.

Becoming Aware of My Powerlessness

I felt I was doing really well in Al-Anon. After all, my husband did go in for treatment. Didn't that mean I was doing something right? Well, he went, but stayed only two days, and my sickness reigned. I would take the truck keys and hide them, keep the checkbook at work so he couldn't write checks, and call throughout the day to be sure he was sober. None of this kept him from drinking. I couldn't control his life nor mine.

One night there was a wreck. I was devastated, but thanks to the little bit of Al-Anon I was able to grasp, I made it through the night. I realized that he couldn't control this disease and I had to leave it alone too. When I fully gave up and let my Higher Power take over, I began to relax. I had to be put in a powerless situation before I realized that I had no control over alcohol or the alcoholic.

Could I really trust in Someone greater than myself? Just at this time I read something that helped me begin to "Let Go and Let God." It said:

"Dear _____,
Thanks, but I don't need your help today.
                              Love, God"

During the next few weeks when I felt I needed to give God a hand, I would take out this sheet of paper and read it. You know something? He's really done great without my help.

Awareness Came When I Was Ready

I was in such delicate shape in the beginning that if the Al-Anon fellowship had been confrontational or dictatorial, I would not have made it. I could easily have been pushed off the edge. I only began dealing with issues when I was ready and able. I believe this is why my Higher Power waited until I had two years of Al-Anon recovery to reveal to me that my father, stepfather, brother, first husband, and many others in my life were all alcoholics. I needed to be gently loved back to life and given the time I needed to listen, relate, and apply what I could.

I have found that the same tools I used to heal from the effects of alcoholism are very useful in other situations I experience. In working on difficult relationships, I begin by applying all Twelve Steps to the relationship. The excellent questions in the back of Al-Anon's book, *The Dilemma of the Alcoholic Marriage*, help me approach the relationship one Step at a time and also to take an inventory of my role. My Sponsor helps me to see where my problem areas lie. Then I do what I can to make my part of the relationship better. This may involve making amends, or perhaps changing my behavior toward the person—more detachment, compassion, or communication; less involvement, or whatever. Healing is likely when I surrender the relationship to the Higher Power and become willing for it to be different. It is no surprise that most often I am the one who changes, not the other person. In time, as I work my program, there are occasionally changes in someone else, too. Could it be because I have let go and am minding my own business?

CHAPTER TWO

Practicing these Principles:
Steps One, Two, and Three

Regardless of the situation that brings new and sometimes unwelcome knowledge to our awareness, a flood
of insight can suddenly overcome us. Revelations spring
up, one after another, until we find ourselves wishing
for a vacation from all this new reality. We may have
the urge to quit, shut down, and stop caring. Though
we never get more than we can handle, we may well get
more than we can control.

Feeling out of control can seem life threatening—
especially for those who have been affected by alcoholism, where so much is out of control. But today we are
not helpless. We can take Al-Anon's First Step, admitting that we are powerless over the facts of our situation
and the other people involved and that our lives have
become unmanageable. In this early stage of awareness,
we may be powerless to do more than find the willingness to look at the truth. Anything beyond that makes
life seem even more unmanageable and overwhelming.
Fortunately, the First Step is not the last.

In times of great stress it can be easy to believe that
there must be a simple solution to the problem that will
restore us to sanity—if we could only win the lottery
or get a divorce, all would be well. We might secretly

wish that an abusive parent would disappear or die, or that a miracle cure for a terminal illness would materialize. We imagine that if only this or that would happen, all our problems would disappear. Turning a particular fantasy solution into a higher power will let us down again and again, just as making an alcoholic loved one into a higher power can only lead to despair. We rarely know why we are faced with problems or what lessons we will learn from the experience. Sometimes it takes a crisis to force us to take the Second Step: we come to believe that our only hope for sanity can be found in a Power greater than ourselves. With the Third Step, we act on this belief; we make a decision to turn our will, our lives, and our circumstances over to the care of that Higher Power.

With the help of these Steps, we learn that alcoholism is a family disease. It thrives on isolation, secrecy, and denial, even when no crisis confronts us. When trouble appears, the last thing we may want to do is talk about it with others. But the only way to release ourselves from the hold of these dark demons is to break the isolation and bring them into the light by sharing with others who understand. It may feel like an enormous risk, but talking honestly about the situation is the key to healing. Although friends, lovers, and family members may not be able to offer a non-judgmental response to these sensitive subjects, most of us find unconditional love and acceptance in Al-Anon, no matter how horrible and blame-worthy we may think we are.

Reflections on Practicing these Principles

Finding the God of My Understanding

I tried to control alcohol and the alcoholic by drinking with him, by trying to outdrink him, by leaving him, by attempting suicide, by crying, by trying to make him jealous, and by trying to be a good wife, a better sex partner, a buddy, and a friend. He still drank. Nothing—absolutely nothing that I did—had any control over alcohol or him. I had withdrawn to the point where I could not meet strangers in a grocery store aisle for fear they would look at me and would see something wrong with me. They might even say something to me, and I just knew I couldn't answer. We had no children, no house, no bank account, and yet I needed that man desperately in my life. I worked and supported him, providing him with money every morning so he could drink while I left the car for him and took the bus to work—yet I needed him. I loved him and I hated him. As Step One says, I had no control over alcohol and my life was unmanageable.

Once I accepted this, Al-Anon encouraged me to believe in a Power greater than myself. I hated this Second Step because it referred to God and I didn't want God. But I had been brought face to face with how helpless and sick I had really become. I had no other choices but to go forward or backward. I knew I would go crazy if I didn't go forward, so I tried. I came to believe in Al-Anon first and the good feeling that I got when I came into the meeting room. Many weeks went by with me saying the Serenity Prayer and referring to Al-Anon as the Power. People also suggested I think about this Higher Power as fate, nature, or anything that is good. It started to work. I turned my will and my life over to Al-Anon, fate, and nature.

My husband and I separated and I was very lonely, very afraid, and wanting to go back to him. I was unable to eat, sleep, or do anything but cry and think about him. Only then, when my Sponsor said, "Are you willing to do anything to feel better," was I ready to answer, "Yes, yes, I'll do anything." She said to ask for help from the God of my understanding. I hated to hear that but knew I had to try, if only to prove her wrong. I said my first sincere prayer: "For God's sake if you are there, help me!" I crawled into bed, cried a few minutes, and fell asleep. My Sponsor reminded me the next day that my prayer had been heard, that I did get some sleep, and that my Higher Power is always there if I want help. I learned to try talking to this God and to look for Him/Her in the blue skies, blossoming flowers, and birds singing in green treetops. Now I realize that God can be found everywhere—in me too.

An Attitude of Gratitude

My husband has heart disease, hypoglycemia, a hiatal hernia, and now emphysema. Throughout all this I have found it so helpful to keep going to the first three Steps of

Al-Anon—I am powerless and my life is unmanageable, but God can restore me to sanity and help me regain my balance. My prayer is, "Please God, help me with what's happening right now." My husband gets angry with me when these physical problems get him down, just as he did before he found recovery in AA. Accepting that I can't make him well is as vital to my serenity as accepting that I can't keep him from drinking. I must release him with love to accept the consequences when he overexerts or fails to take his medication. In this, too, I must let him have the dignity of his own choices.

Along with poor health came a deterioration of a normal sex life. Our doctors have been helpful and understanding, but we both have had to accept that this is the way it is (and has been for ten years). Being grateful for the good life we do have, the love we share, and our respective programs has made it possible for us to be happy with the intimacy we *can* have instead of bemoaning what we *can't* have. Our lives are full—we have children and grandchildren, our meetings, and Twelfth Step work, as well as Al-Anon and AA conferences. I try hard to have an attitude of gratitude.

Tools for Coping with Awareness
I could not trust my husband, an alcoholic who was actively drinking, when he said the affair he'd been having was over. My imagination began to go absolutely wild, picturing everything that ever went on between them. I felt frozen. I could not even cry. I sat on the couch, paralyzed and numb, whenever he was not home,

until I could not stand my obsession. I could not let it go. Finally, I told myself something had to change because I was crazy. From that day on I began attending Al-Anon regularly.

I had to force myself to get well, and this is what I did. I wrote down a list of what I needed to do: attend a minimum of two meetings a week, get a Sponsor I could talk to, and chair a meeting once a month. I talked on the phone about my pain. It had to come out. Soon I was able to cry again, and even though I still felt bad, I was at least beginning to feel.

I attended open AA meetings and began to realize that infidelity often went along with the disease of alcoholism. My husband was an unhappy person looking for something to make him feel better. Eventually, I made the connection that I, too, was looking for someone (my husband) to make me happy. I began to understand that his being involved with anyone else really had nothing to do with me. I stopped feeling like such an undesirable loser.

I still carried the hate for him and this other woman, but as I became more immersed in the Al-Anon program, I began to work the Steps. I was powerless over my husband's behavior, and it was his choice whether or not to honor his wedding vows. I was grateful I honored mine, so I wouldn't have to carry the guilt of an affair with me. The only entry in our *One Day at a Time in Al-Anon* book that deals with forgiveness says that we can only forgive ourselves for judging someone in the first place. Even though I thought my husband's behavior was wrong, I had not walked in his shoes.

Many nights his presence was unaccounted for, but I believed that "Knowledge, if it is meant to come to you, will do so." In other words, mind my own business. I stopped asking him questions when I knew his answers would be lies and I stopped searching for information that would bring me pain. I concentrated on the solution—Al-Anon—instead of the problem.

A year and a half later my husband sought treatment. Only a week after his return, he told me he had gone to see the other woman. I sat quietly and said nothing, for which I will always be grateful. His next words were, "She has cancer of the throat." My only response was, "You might want to say a prayer for her, because that's a disease that kills." As I heard those words come from my lips, I knew I had accepted complete powerlessness and that my insecurity and jealously had been removed.

Today I am able to talk about my gratitude for this woman who entered our lives. I am glad that the pain was so great I felt forced to *live* the Al-Anon program, not just learn about it.

Courage to Share

Because I had been so deeply affected by having been molested when I was young, that was the biggest deterrent to my recovery in Al-Anon. How could I recover spiritually and mentally and believe that Al-Anon and God loved me, when I felt so filthy? My earliest recollection of being molested was when I was about age two. I believed such things didn't happen to good girls.

One night at a meeting, I gathered the courage to bring up this problem. I was sure that after I told my story, the members would feel nothing but disgust for me. Instead, they loved me enough to open old wounds of their own to reassure me that I was not an abominable thing, but lovable and worthy of love. Because of their love and sharing, I was able to deal with this nightmare that had haunted me most of my life.

At a recent meeting, the problem was brought up again. I said to God, "Please, not again. I want to forget it. I don't want to hurt any more." Then I proceeded to share. Al-Anon has given me the courage and strength to continue to face this distasteful subject. I know that my own experience is not an isolated case.

Admitting Powerlessness

I had a girlfriend to whom I was attracted, but at the same time I wanted to leave. I had little self-worth or belief in myself after growing up in an alcoholic home where I had no say, where I was told my feelings were wrong or inappropriate, and where their expression was met with punishment. So I looked only to my girlfriend's faults. I argued with her, criticized her, and tried to leave, but when she cried I felt sorry for her and apologized. I felt trapped, unable to make changes in my life. After some time, we married. While our relationship had good times, we also argued violently. I had never known how to relate to girls and now had trouble coping with being married.

I felt a sense of powerlessness over the direction my

life took and didn't know what I was feeling. I only knew I was confused. I reacted rather than acted. My life was unmanageable. Fortunately, my brother in AA directed me to Al-Anon.

I learned there that my reactions to situations and people were my attempts to exercise power over them and to control my life. I found my efforts to change my wife into the person I wanted exhausting, non-productive, and destructive to our relationship. I learned in Al-Anon that I could not exercise power over anyone but myself. I had no power over my father, including his drinking and his behavior. Nor did I have any right to try to exercise power over him. And he has no power over me! I learned of my first freedom. I began by not reacting to criticism of my actions or ideas. Step One was the beginning of learning to "Live and Let Live."

Steps One, Two, and Three

Not long after we were legally separated, I heard that my husband, a drug addict and alcoholic, had held up a store. I didn't want to go home because I thought he was going to come after me with a gun. I knew he was angry. He couldn't understand why I broke up the family.

That night I grabbed onto my Higher Power and, like a baby, got into His imaginary arms. It may seem ridiculous, but to me it was real. I went through the night without a care, and when I awoke I was able to think better. I was grateful for the First Step—that I could admit how powerless I was over this incident. I was not at fault for what my husband did.

Many of his letters while incarcerated were ugly and angry. I was afraid. I wished he wouldn't get out, but I knew that was unrealistic. I thank God for the Al-Anon program because it brings me back to reality. When he did get out, I didn't want him to take our children to see his family, but Al-Anon helped me to let go of my resentments. I let go. After all, his family is their family too.

Powerless over Others

I was determined to hang on to my husband, drunk or not, and the only way I felt I could do that was to be perfect. The house sparkled, I prepared meals in the haute cuisine class, our wash was the brightest, I was ever ready to make love, the snow was cleared in winter, and the yard groomed and bloomed in summer. The more I aspired for perfection, the more my husband found fault and the more I feared he would walk out.

I was becoming worn out from all I was doing, and my fear of being alone was eating me alive. After I fell apart in my neighbor's kitchen, she took me to my first Al-Anon meeting. Many meetings later, I grasped the idea that the only person I have any power over is myself. If my husband decided to leave me, I wouldn't be able to stop him. Next I turned to my Higher Power for guidance in His will, not mine. It didn't happen overnight, but eventually I stopped being afraid my husband might leave me. With Al-Anon in my life, I believe I will never be alone again.

Breaking the Silence

I am an incest survivor—notice that I did not say "victim." I believe that once a person starts dealing with abuse from the past in the alcoholic home, one starts giving up the label of victim. I use the Twelve Steps and Traditions to deal with this issue.

It has been crucial for me to stand up and speak out—to break the silence. I am a survivor. There is hope, there is help, and I have the inalienable right to human dignity. I will never let anyone take that away from me again.

Turning It Over

I joined Al-Anon before my husband hit bottom. Sobriety did not bring him health. It exposed serious complications, one of which was depression. When my partner discovered he could no longer learn new skills nor assimilate new knowledge, he despaired of ever working again. If I had not practiced living one day at a time then, I would have been unable to cope. Throughout his several attempts at suicide, I constantly applied the Steps, at times feeling I would never progress beyond Step Three. Since I have now handed over all decisions to my Higher Power, life is more peaceful.

Seeking Help

Five years into our marriage, as my husband's drinking increased, he became extremely abusive. I sought help from a family physician and psychiatrist, but the doctors couldn't help me and I felt hopeless. During a violent episode, I escaped—in total panic—to a friend's home, where I was introduced to Al-Anon literature. I then attempted to work the program alone with the literature—an impossible task. After a month, I went to my first meeting in desperation. I was amazed: they knew how I felt; they even expressed my feelings! My dam, built up from years of abuse in two marriages, broke wide open. The pain, bruises, anger, and broken dreams poured out in tears. I hurt so bad inside, I couldn't speak. They offered their shoulders, their hugs, their understanding, and their time. Al-Anon was my life preserver. My husband's response was escalated violence and mental abuse. At the suggestion of some Al-Anon friends, I went to a center for battered women.

Gradually, with Al-Anon's help, I started living again. I learned to detach, to see the mental and spiritual aspects of his illness, and to realize that his words were totally irrational. Nothing I said or did could change that. When he later joined AA, I was full of hope, but as I watched him regress mentally and spiritually again, I turned him over to God.

When violence erupted again, this time at our dog, my Higher Power was with me as my daughter and I escaped into a snowstorm. My Sponsor took us in until I could get into a safe house. All I had was my daughter, my Al-Anon book, my car, and the clothes we were wearing. I could no longer deny my responsibility for the safety of myself and my daughter.

Today, two years later, having relocated, I have gone back to school and am working. I am raising my child as a single parent, free of the fear of violence. My problems are not solved, only changed. I have my fears, lack of money, loneliness, and a lack of time, but I feel directed now to use my talents to the fullest and to see my problems as opportunities for growth.

Taking Step Three

An hour after my boss informed me that "I didn't have a future" with the company, my wife of 17 years called to say she had filed for divorce. How numb I felt, standing in my office, the phone receiver in my hand. I remembered hearing in Al-Anon that our Higher Power doesn't give us more than we can handle. For the first time in my five years of actively working the Al-Anon program, I thought they had lied. Yet the inner voice kept repeating that it just couldn't be a random occurrence that I had been hit by these two bombshells within an hour of one another. My Higher Power had to be involved somehow. A surge of anger overcame me: How could He do this to me? It took a loving Sponsor to help me understand, during the ensuing months, that the "to me" in this question was ego. Either I was going to run the show, or my Higher Power was. I took the Third Step and decided to turn my will and my life over to this Higher Power's care.

I moved out of my house, away from my family, and into a transient hotel. Although I had my Al-Anon program, my Al-Anon friends, and my Higher Power, I had never felt so alone. I found myself making 3:00 a.m. calls to very understanding Al-Anon friends who let me talk and cry. They lovingly told me the things I needed to hear to get me through the next five minutes of the next hour of the next 24 hours. I went to lots of meetings. I read and read and re-read the literature. Most importantly, I stayed in close contact with my Sponsor, who had taught me that working a program is like saving in a bank: you have to make ongoing spiritual deposits for that rainy day when you need to make a big withdrawal.

Sharing My Own Truth

I did not ask to be born into a family affected by two generations of alcoholism. Neither did I make a conscious decision to be attracted to members of my own sex. Nonetheless, both these situations became apparent to me at an early age, as did the fact that I needed to keep my mouth shut about both of them.

In my family, talking about reality was not encouraged. In addition we were expected to maintain impossibly high standards of conduct and "success." Because of the intense focus on appearances, the only effective tool I found for conforming was dishonesty. At the time, I thought I was the only liar in the bunch. I felt deeply shamed and inadequate.

In this environment, the wonderful, benevolent, mysterious Higher Power of my early childhood gradually gave way to God the Judge—a stern, crabby, old bureaucrat whose notice it was best to avoid. The feelings that I had developed toward other men, which felt so natural to me, were presented at the top of the list of things that God hated, so that my very existence seemed an insult to God. I believed this and opted for atheism.

Fifteen years later, after an emotional crisis, the Higher Power I had turned my back on arranged for me to find Al-Anon. There I became re-acquainted with my spirituality and with my right to a Higher Power. In my Fourth Step, I discovered that I had values that I had chosen to ignore or deny in order to please others or because it seemed the "easy" way. I learned not to worry so much about what others thought of me, but to pay attention to what I thought was right. I found that I had to surrender every area of my life to my Higher Power, even my sexuality.

Today, at least in Al-Anon, I can be candid about my sexual orientation. Not everyone who receives this information is comfortable with it, but no one has told me to be quiet or to leave. I do not feel the need to distance myself from those who have a hard time dealing with my homosexuality. I have come to see that I not only became sick and unhappy by my reaction to alcoholism, but also by my reaction to homophobia, and I can recover in both areas through the loving principles of Al-Anon and my joyful friendship with God.

Reaching Out

I was 16 years old and wanted to die. I tried to kill myself several times but never succeeded. I guess it wasn't time for me to die, or I really didn't want death, just attention. You see, my dad is an alcoholic. After I discovered Alateen, I realized that I wasn't the only one in the world with this problem. With these people here to listen and help me out, I really feel better. I know I can't help my dad, but I no longer want to be dead because I know that I can help myself and others too.

Whenever I feel troubled, hurt, or alone, I try to remember to speak out and let people know. I have always been led to someone who was willing to help.

Finding Love and Support in Al-Anon

Ten years ago I cracked up and clobbered my kid. Two weeks earlier, a whole volcano of lost memories and feelings about growing up in a violent alcoholic family had begun erupting. One memory kept haunting me—the worst beating I ever received as a child: razor straps, broomsticks, and constant verbal abuse. I couldn't get rid of the memory. Then I repeated history with my own kid. I didn't see the connection for weeks. Meanwhile my two girls were whisked off to foster care and I started psychiatric treatment, which eventually led me to Al-Anon.

The first night in Al-Anon, I blurted out my whole story. When I realized I was the only one among them with children in foster care, I didn't speak at a meeting for the next two years. I did listen, though, and gradually realized that among these people there was really nothing to fear. They knew the facts and still accepted me. It was their constant, continuous loving of me, just the way I was, that brought me back into this world again. In the beginning I felt like a little child with so much to learn. It was that feeling of being loved and cared for in Al-Anon that gave me a second chance at life.

Other People's Opinions

My husband is serving a five-year sentence for molesting a child. It was more than I could bear, and I left him. But you can't successfully run away from your problems. After some counseling, I returned to the country home we had loved so much. I knew if I were ever to have any peace, I must forgive him.

It hasn't been easy staying in the area where his offense was public knowledge. I quit attending a church where I felt uncomfortable. Finally, knowing I had to have human companionship, I went back to my Al-Anon group. It is hard to keep your anonymity in the place you grew up. I had known some of the members for years. But I felt the complete love and acceptance of our group, who know the real meaning of the word "friendship." With their support I'm beginning to come out of my shell and live again.

My husband seems to have embraced the AA way of life and I am eagerly awaiting his release from prison. I know there will be places we will never be accepted, even in our own family, but as long as we have our Twelve Steps and Traditions we can make it.

Sharing the Dark Secrets

I found that not only was incest a taboo, but talking about it among uninformed friends was too. It happened when I was of kindergarten age—my brother sexually molested me on a weekly basis. The part of my alcoholic family that knew about it shunned me. My mother still believes I want to break up the family because I chose to seek help for the hurt.

Thank God for my loving Al-Anon group, who listened to what I had to say without judgment. Their acceptance helped me detach and not take on anybody else's feelings toward incest, particularly my family's. I found a haven from the storm of feelings I was going through. It helped me keep my feet on the ground and provided the unconditional love that others weren't able to give. I was freed from the bondage of a constant sense of loneliness. I had always felt different from everyone. Recurring bouts of depression and an overall nagging feeling of worthlessness and self-doubt had doggedly followed me in my adult life, largely from carrying the burden of the "secret" that I had been too terrified to tell. I know now that I was right to seek help and that it is possible to feel good again. I no longer have to play the role of "different" because I no longer have to hide.

I Have Choices

Over time my husband's abusive behavior and constant put-downs pounded the tiny bit of self-worth I had pulled together into the ground. I saw myself as a victim. It was now peace at any price. I tried to appease, amuse, pamper—anything to try to delay the displays of temper. Then I decided to get back at him and opted for divorce. I soon discovered that divorce doesn't necessarily end a relationship. After months of promises and dreams of a new life together, we remarried. The downward spiral continued. The despair I felt cannot be put into words.

After a familiar argument one night, I left the room

and lit one of the three million cigarettes I smoked then. I said to myself, or God, or somebody, or nobody, "What is going on here? There is a pattern. What is it?" I looked up, and—as God is my witness—from the ceiling I "saw" the word "alcoholism" float to the floor. I couldn't believe it—and I still can't.

The wellness part of my journey has without question come from God. I tried every method, read every book and then some, and still could not pick up the pieces of my damaged self-worth. Through what I choose to believe is His grace, I was led to Al-Anon, to specific individuals, and to ideas that could lead me out of the quagmire. I learned one of my most important lessons early—that I have choices. This recognition opened avenues to me that I never knew existed: it was my real beginning.

I have now reached a place on my journey where I will no longer tolerate unacceptable behavior. I love my husband very deeply but can no longer accept an abusive lifestyle. I have gained enough self-worth to give him to God. I can't help him. I can love him, but I can't help him.

Part Two
Acceptance

CHAPTER THREE

Seeing in a New Way

Major changes can shatter the beliefs we hold most dear about ourselves, our loved ones, and the world we live in. No wonder we feel so vulnerable, so confused, when the very foundation on which we've built our lives seems to be crumbling beneath us. Although we may no longer deny reality, many of us experience a deep sense of loss as we let go of the make believe world that kept us feeling safe.

The loss of a dream can sometimes be even more painful than tangible loss. How many of us have fallen in love with someone's potential? How many have desperately clung to promises that next time would be different—the drinking would stop, the abusive behavior would never be repeated—only to be disappointed again and again? We often have such worthy and generous hopes for our loved ones and for ourselves. We dream of success and fulfillment in our home lives and our work. We fervently wish to leave a burdensome past behind. Whether or not these dreams are realistic, when something happens to crush them, we lose a part of ourselves. We may feel frustrated, confused, and terribly impotent when old ideas and solutions don't work. It is as if we were trapped in a hallway with no doors or windows.

Rage, fear, and other unsettling feelings can arise.

For anyone who is unaccustomed to such emotions, this experience can be especially frightening. After a lifetime of ducking unpleasant feelings, or of having those feelings mocked or dismissed, most of us fear that we won't survive them. The problem is that stuffed feelings don't just disappear. We can carry them around with us for years. Sometimes our only hope for release from this increasingly oppressive burden is to sit still and feel the feelings. At such times, sharing with an Al-Anon Sponsor who knows the details of our situation can be a great relief. A Sponsor can help us remember that we are not alone. He or she may point out an Al-Anon principle or tool that can help us put our overwhelming feelings into perspective. This ongoing support often helps us discover ways we might never have considered to express or release these feelings. In time, with this help from other Al-Anon members, many of us feel better prepared to determine and take whatever actions our circumstances require.

Reflections on Seeing in a New Way

Managing My Pain

There's a branch of medicine called "pain management" that offers techniques to ease the pain of chronic
and terminal illness. For me, there's a form of treatment
to alleviate emotional pain: it's called Al-Anon.

When I came to Al-Anon I sought relief from the
constant ache of living with an active, abusive drinker.
I thought if I could just remove the alcoholic, the pain
would disappear. At my first meeting I knew help was
on the way when I heard from others like myself who
were suffering from the destructive effects of the disease
of alcoholism. After only a few visits it became apparent
that there were many antidotes—the Steps, prayer and
meditation, the Serenity Prayer, and the slogans, just to
name a few.

After years of remission (joy and well-being, actually),
another painful period surfaced. When my sister died, an
old wound reopened and I faced many of the hurts of my
childhood. I didn't think I could bear the grief. But once
again I was surrounded by soothing and healing love and
acceptance. Al-Anon not only gave me the tools to go
through that pain, it enabled me to grow through it.

Two years ago there was another flare-up of pain. I discovered my daughter's alcoholism after she nearly killed

herself in an automobile accident. The distress was so pervasive, I felt like a newcomer—confused and hurting. But once again, others took care of me when I didn't feel capable of helping myself. No one asked me to deny the pain, they just reminded me of the tools for recovery.

As much as I'd like to avoid pain, it's a fact of life. Before Al-Anon, I used destructive forms of pain management, such as denial and avoidance. I covered up the wounds without treating them; I even tried to touch up the x-rays. Once in Al-Anon, I not only learned how to manage my pain, I learned how to transform it into a spiritual advantage, to grow in compassion and understanding, and to apply it to the benefit of myself and others.

Feeling Uncomfortable Feelings

The thought that he was hitting his bottom was perhaps the only saving grace for me during the horrendous experience of waiting for a verdict and subsequently a sentence to be imposed upon my alcoholic son. Hope reigned that recovery would eventually restore him to a normal way of life. At the same time I felt grief and anguish, which I allowed myself the privilege of expressing in tears each day for the first couple of months of his imprisonment. Tears were important and natural under the circumstances, and having an Al-Anon Sponsor who fully agreed certainly made all the difference. Little by little, tears came less and less, but then came the old symptom—the nagging inner voice that said, "Do something! Send him literature, tapes…" The hardest thing was to do nothing, or rather to be still and let an answer come. Hitting bottom means different things to different people at different times, and I was gently led to hit another bottom of my own. I saw that I had to trust my son's recovery to a Power greater than myself. In that willingness came serenity, courage, some wisdom, and freedom from the effects of his disease.

Grieving the Loss of a Dream

For two years I had tried to start a family; finally, I believed I was pregnant. Needless to say I was over-joyed to share my hopeful news with my husband. I was totally unprepared for the shocks to come. My husband had been drinking and told me all the things that were wrong with me and our marriage, and that it was my responsibility to make him fall back in love with me. I knew my husband sometimes had a problem with alcohol but thought it wasn't serious. I knew nothing about the disease.

In the weeks that followed, I lost the baby; it was a tubal pregnancy. I was a mass of fear, insecurity, pain, and much confusion. I could not understand how I could have made so many mistakes. By the time I entered Al-Anon, I couldn't get out of bed, brush my teeth, *and* get dressed; each morning I chose whether to brush my teeth or get dressed.

Once in the Al-Anon program, I went through another period of grief. In death there is a finality that one has no choice but to accept, but my grief is over the loss of an ideal, and there is opportunity for denial and pain at every new crisis. I lost my illusion of my husband, and, more painful, the hopes for a family and a sane marriage of two people working as a team.

I had to give up the "poor me's," the "whys," the "buts," and the "ifs." I had to accept that I am powerless over alcoholism. I had to use the Serenity Prayer, talk to my Sponsor, and share my grief. I know now that the grief I experience is normal, whether it is over the loss of a job, a pet, a home, or an illusion. As long as my life is involved with alcoholism, I will probably go through periods of grief. But if I use the tools of the program, I will be able to work through it.

Learning to Express Emotions

As a child I was very shy. I could not talk with anyone or show any affection. I was too ashamed of the situation in my alcoholic home. My father, when drunk, seemed to have a compulsion to threaten us with a gun. We hid the guns but somehow he always found one. He would load it, cock it, and point it at us with threats to kill us all. When I was a teenager, after a particularly ugly episode, I decided to kill my father. I got a gun and was on my way to do so when my mother intervened and persuaded me not to ruin my life. To this day I do not know if I could have done it. I do know I am very thankful that I did not.

One rainy night, my alcoholic brother shot himself in the head. I remember a coldly clinical discussion I had with the mortician about the difficulty of making my brother cosmetically presentable because of such a head wound. I showed no emotion. I did not shed a tear at my brother's funeral.

Later, in adulthood, although elated over having children after 12 childless years, I could not express any of the emotion I felt. I did not hold or hug our children. This was a loss to all of us. I was not a whole person. I was emotionally crippled. I had been involved in church work for many years and was deeply religious—but not very spiritual. Out of my desperation, I prayed for guidance and help. In retrospect, I think that this was my first genuine prayer.

Just two days later, an Al-Anon member came into my life and I started on my road to recovery. At my first Al-Anon meeting, the speaker related many experiences that I found painful to think about. I think I was like the ugly caterpillar who saw a beautiful butterfly floating happily along on the breeze and said, "You'll never get me up in a thing like that." After each meeting I would feel much better about myself. It soon became clear that each time I missed two meetings in a row, I would have a slip and start my negative thinking again. I listened to Al-Anon members expressing their feelings honestly, and I began to face my own feelings and to talk about them.

A helpful exercise was to write two letters to my dead parents, the first to express some of my anger and resentments, the second to express my love and appreciation to them as my parents.

Through counseling, much reading, and working the Al-Anon program, I have learned to express my emotions and my love for people. I have accepted that I am a person of worth and that many people genuinely like me, even love me. I have learned to give warm, affectionate hugs, and it really feels great. I find that the deep, hidden anger is largely gone and that it has been replaced with thoughts of love, compassion, caring, understanding, and gratitude. My wife, children, and friends all have told me of the great and remarkable changes they see in me. I have found that I love life.

Becoming Honest with Myself

Have you ever heard that people can't change the truth, but the truth can change people? I believe that this is what has happened to me. I had an awful time with the Serenity Prayer. I thought to accept the things I cannot change meant I had to like them. I finally realized I don't have to like them one bit, only recognize them for what they are, and accept the reality of what is. My, that made a difference! I became willing to become honest with myself, and I have changed. I don't know just exactly how or when. I only know I have, and I'm so grateful because I know the changes that have taken place in me are good ones.

My comprehension was slow at times, but repetition is a terrific learning tool. I am not grateful that I was married to an alcoholic, but I am grateful that the experience opened the doors of Al-Anon to me. I found that by attending meetings and reading Al-Anon literature, it was nearly impossible for me not to grow and change as a person given a little time.

A Safe Place for Feelings

During my early childhood, active alcoholism was present in our home. Much of the abuse I felt was neglect. Punishment was by solitary confinement. I learned early not to talk.

My dad put me down a lot, along with other people. He called them "chumps," "dummies," and "low class." I would cringe, ache, and hurt, but not speak. I was afraid of what his tongue could do: belittle, denigrate, downgrade, humiliate, demean, and crush. I thought he was brilliant.

One night, in an alcoholic daze, my father pushed my mother down the stairs. Nobody said anything about it. I stuffed my feelings of horror and fear.

Because of this background, I didn't have the emotional resources for dealing with the experiences I faced as an adult: verbal, emotional, and finally intolerable physical abuse and divorce.

In Al-Anon I have found, at last, a safe place to learn to express feelings in an appropriate way. When others share in meetings, I gain insight into my own feelings. The encouragement to share, the freedom to speak, and the reasoning things out together are wonderful. Fear, anger, resentment, and hostility are being replaced by joy, faith, acceptance, and contentment.

After "the Worst" Has Happened

My husband was drinking heavily and on disability leave from work. None of the doctors he saw for seven months diagnosed the disease of alcoholism. The "what ifs" were eating away at me constantly. What if they fired him? What if our friends and family found out? We had debts that my salary couldn't pay, and his child support was months in arrears. What if he was arrested for nonpayment? I was edgy, fearful, frantic, and depressed.

When the letter came and he was let go, my chief reaction was relief. The other shoe had fallen, and I could start taking action. I was also relieved that others finally validated my opinion—my husband did have a drinking problem. I had to truly face and accept the First Step. Nothing I had done—all the enabling, supporting, driving to doctors, picking up prescriptions, etc.—had stopped the inevitable. Do you know what? It was okay! And so was I! Once it happened, I was set free. I could turn the focus on myself.

I started making progress in Al-Anon, enough that I was able to leave a job full of stress and misdirection and find one that gave me respect and challenge. When I was ready to make the change, my Higher Power put me in touch with the right people and the new job appeared.

Sometimes the worst "what if" has to happen before change can come about. And the "what if" is often worse than the "what happens." Even if the "what happens" is as bad as I feared, the Al-Anon program, the people in it, and my Higher Power are there to help me through it.

Facing the Legacy of Alcoholism

Something was very wrong with my relationship with my father. I have disturbing memories, especially one of a time when he got into bed with me, drunk, when I was about seven. I pretended to be asleep, but he said, in slurred words, "You know I love you," and reached toward me. The memory stops abruptly right there. I don't know how much or how little may be hiding behind it, but I have felt acute uneasiness about it for years, and I'm afraid there may be other events I don't remember. I have many vivid memories of my father's drunken behavior—speeding cars, smashed furniture, family fights—but that one incident troubles me more than all the rest.

I never heard anyone talk about my father's drinking, though his craziness was apparent to us all. Even now I have to fight feelings of disloyalty and betrayal in order to talk about these things with my Al-Anon friends. I still need to resist thinking "it wasn't that bad." I experience fears that threaten to overwhelm the real but still fragile self-respect and wholeness I've gained in Al-Anon. I get paralyzing childhood terrors of "the thing" outside the door. Worse are my inner suspicions that I "asked for it" in some way, inviting my father's inappropriate and unwanted sexual advances. Having grown up around the disease of alcoholism, I am only too ready to believe that I am an evil, worthless person. Yet I find nothing but warm acceptance and understanding from Al-Anon members. They have helped me to learn that my feelings are important and need to be accepted. But feelings aren't facts. When my feelings tell me that all is hopeless, I can remember that even though I have been affected by alcoholism, the Al-Anon program provides a path to recovery that works.

I guess my Higher Power has been gently preparing me to be able to face this legacy. The Twelve Steps, the slogans, and the loving support I receive in Al-Anon have given me the strength I need. Miraculously, I am now in a very loving relationship, full of respect and compassion. Though my past has left me with a very distorted understanding of the place of sexuality in love, I'm beginning to grow in that area too.

Surviving Loss

An older couple I met through Al-Anon unofficially adopted my family, and we adopted them, going on picnics together and sharing holidays. I began calling them "Mamma" and "Poppa," and they called my husband and me "The Kids." They became the parents I had always wanted but never had.

One night Poppa called with the news that Mama was in the hospital. Moments later she was dead. No one close to me had ever died. I was shattered.

For months I was sad and withdrawn. I did not want to go to meetings or be around people. My husband and family tried to comfort me, and Al-Anon friends came to see me, but I pushed them all away. I became more and more depressed, feeling that my Higher Power had left me.

Despite my rudeness, my family and friends stuck by me. My Al-Anon friends helped me look at myself. They insisted that I go to meetings. Finally, I started writing down my thoughts and talking to my Sponsor again. I began using the Steps in this difficult situation. Today I thank God that Mamma and Poppa were put in my life. They taught me so much about love and living "One Day at a Time." Now I'm living what they helped me learn.

Accepting Emotions

I used to think that being a member of Al-Anon meant I was supposed to be in control of my emotions at all times. But I have found that it's normal to get angry sometimes. It's okay to be hurt when someone says something to hurt me. After years of living with alcoholism, I had plenty of feelings of guilt, anger, and jealousy. Al-Anon meetings and a supportive Sponsor helped me to look at them and to accept and forgive myself.

I had to deal with fear in telling my spouse what I think a relationship is. I had to learn to share my feelings about our sex life. I had to risk the fear of rejection. To do this, I had to turn to my Higher Power. I had to have faith that if it was meant for us to be together, then God would give us the ability to understand and accept each other.

I also have had to look at my ability to accept my spouse's feelings without anger, resentment, or hurt. He is just as frail as I am. I have had to take time to listen and think about what he says without reacting immediately, especially if it is a feeling he is sharing. This has been one of the most beautiful experiences I have ever had. It's like a rose unfolding with dewdrops falling down the petals.

With the help of the Al-Anon program, I am living one day at a time. I am also married one day at a time. This simplifies my life.

Releasing Resentment

It's hard to raise children, especially stubborn ones. It is even harder when the family has been affected by the disease of alcoholism. My son is disabled and the most defiant of my three children. He learned to use his disability to get what he wanted. In fighting with my son and in my confusion I developed resentment towards him and his problems. I didn't feel love, and I felt guilty for this lack.

The Serenity Prayer kept reminding me to accept the things I could not change. So I accepted my feelings without judgment, realizing that resentment blocks love. I asked God to help me to love him. At night I told each of the children, individually, that I loved them. I had to fake it with my son at first, feeling empty, but I didn't fight it. After a while, the resentment started easing away and I didn't feel so hollow any more. God was replacing it with love. My son and I started communicating and I started accepting him as the unique individual he is. It became easier to accept others as well.

After a stay in the hospital, my son and I started pushing one another again. He felt I should wait on him and give him complete attention, as the nurses had. I did, until I realized what I was doing—the same old merry-go-round! But with God's help and Al-Anon's, I'll try again.

Coping with Confusion

Being told so many times by the alcoholic, in effect, that the sky was green and the grass blue, I feared I was losing my mind. Every contradiction scrambled my brains. My days and nights were filled with mixed messages. In some ways it was like being in a foreign country and understanding just a tiny bit of the language: I had to work so hard to find what was real. The longer this went on, the more addled I became. Even today, after years in Al-Anon, when the alcoholic behavior resurfaces, I feel my old fear of losing my mind return. That's when I know I have to double up on whatever I'm doing in the program—and fast.

Questioning Long-Held Spiritual Beliefs

Years before I came into Al-Anon, my spiritual philosophy was in place. Heavy involvement in Al-Anon served to reinforce it. The moment my mother passed away, however, my sense of having a spiritual center evaporated. I began to question beliefs I had had for more than a decade about death and dying and the soul being immortal. Was there really a Higher Power or did life and death happen at random? The earth has been around for billions of years: what was the significance of any one human life? A different aspect of my brain admonished me for doubting the conclusions I had drawn years before. Then I'd say, "Yes, but...."

My grief may have drowned out *my* beliefs but not those of my Al-Anon daughter, my Sponsor, and my Al-Anon friends. Their non-judgmental compassion was a constant source of strength as I plowed my way through the grieving process. Eventually I re-embraced the spiritual tenets I dearly wanted to believe. The spiritual strength of others in Al-Anon contributed significantly to my rediscovering an inner peace.

Leaving Guilt Behind

I came to my first Al-Anon meeting carrying the heavy burden of guilt. If my son turned to alcohol and drugs, then I felt I had failed as a parent. If he had an uncontrollable compulsion to drink, then I had not given him a firm enough foundation. When I covered his bad checks or believed what he told me, then I had enabled him to continue feeding his disease. So no matter which way I turned, I felt guilty. Only by sharing my feelings could I hope to get help for myself.

I learned that alcoholism is a disease; I have no control over it, and neither does he. Everything I had done for him, I did for love. I knew no other behavior, but with the help of my friends in Al-Anon, I now know there is another way. I must love him enough to turn him over to a Higher Power.

Letting the Feelings Out

As the family disease of alcoholism progressed, I learned to bury feelings of inadequacy, confusion, and hurt. As one consequence, I developed physical illnesses, beginning with migraine headaches. When I found out that whatever condition I had developed was not terminal, the symptoms disappeared from that area, only to show up somewhere else. This went on for years. I became a classic hypochondriac.

After coming to Al-Anon, seeking professional help, and reading everything I could get my hands on concerning alcoholism, I began to let some of the feelings come up. I saw that I was so angry I needed to show everyone how tough-minded I was—that I would let no one walk on me. Fear was what I really felt, but I had showed the world how tough I was so many times that I heard my echo and believed it. I thought everyone in Al-Anon would be like me, and then I heard, "I like myself just the way I am." I didn't, and I was confused. I didn't want to change—to let go of the toughness and to deal with the fear—because I was so afraid of disappointment. I might fall apart.

Al-Anon has helped me begin to take some risks. With the help of the Steps, I am looking more honestly at my feelings and accepting what I see. It helps me to share what I discover with my Al-Anon support system, but I am not obligated to justify myself to anyone; it is really between God and me.

I'm learning to treat myself as if I'm valuable. I find that when I practice long enough, I begin to believe it.

Allowing Myself to Grieve

Right now the only way I can bear my loneliness is to force myself to remember what is was like just a few years ago. I'd been in Al-Anon a number of years, living with a man I loved so much yet dying inside because he was killing himself with drink. I knew I had to protect myself

both physically—from his occasional bursts of violence—and also financially, for he had lost his job and I
had to rely on my own earnings. In Al-Anon meetings I
heard some members talk about separation and divorce,
usually in tears. They didn't seem too happy about their
decisions, so I postponed making one. But eventually
my husband started hallucinating during the night. I
got very little sleep and feared I might lose my job, too.
He moved out, but would phone at all hours and sometimes come banging on the outside of the house. Finally,
although I didn't want to, I did what I had to do for me.
I got a restraining order and filed for divorce.

My eyes were red most of the time. I missed him terribly. The house seemed to have an echo without him
there. In the months that followed, I felt good one day
and lousy the next. Then one day I got a call from his
sister: he was dead of an alcoholic seizure.

I know some people, even Al-Anon friends, haven't
been able to understand my grief for a man I divorced.
For me, though, loving him did not stop with divorce,
and it hasn't stopped with death. I remind myself when
I feel as if I'll fall apart that this too shall pass, and I
usually call an Al-Anon friend. I continue to do what
I need for myself—go to meetings, share about my feelings, and try to apply the Steps to my experience. I ask
myself, where is my life unmanageable? What am I powerless over? Where do I need to be restored to sanity by
my Higher Power? And so on. Also, I try to remember
that my husband's Higher Power knew what was best for
him.

Taking Responsibility for My Feelings

When I first started in Al-Anon I thought feelings were forced on me by the outside world. I used expressions like: This makes me so angry! It made me furious! You made me lose control when you did that! You hurt my feelings! These were convenient little sayings to assign someone else the responsibility for how I was feeling. I certainly didn't want responsibility—feelings were bad and should be avoided! I learned that well in the alcoholic home of my childhood.

Although I had accepted responsibility for myself in the early days in Al-Anon, the actual owning of my feelings came two years later, after much patience on the part of my Higher Power. I have concluded that to change the way I live, I first have to change the way I think about it, then change the way I speak about it! Therefore I can no longer say, "You, he, she, it makes me...anything." I can no longer excuse myself from my life. I must say: "I felt hurt because I thought...," or "I felt angry when you...," or "I am happy when we...," and I can only get better with practice! I try very hard not to beat myself up when I can't express my feelings—progress, not perfection. Self-expression is a very important tool, and if I choose not to use it, then I stand in the way of my own recovery and victimize myself.

No one can make me do or feel anything that I don't want to do or feel! That frees me from the burden of not knowing what I *should* feel and places the emphasis on what I *am* feeling. My feelings are neither right nor wrong but are important by virtue of being mine. I have a right to express them in a diplomatic, caring way.

CHAPTER FOUR

Responsibility and Detachment

The family disease of alcoholism blurs our sense of reality, making it difficult to distinguish what is our responsibility and what is not. Some of us avoid taking responsibility, depending on others to take care of our obligations. Some of us become enablers, doing for others what they should be permitted to do for themselves. A false sense of responsibility, which whispers that we are totally and eternally to blame, can keep us from gaining any perspective on our circumstances. Detachment with love sometimes means loving ourselves enough to suspend blame, fear, guilt, and self-pity long enough to separate the problem from ourselves, until we can clarify our options and responsibilities, identify how we are contributing to the problem, and let go of the rest.

However, detachment can be a very uncomfortable process. In situations beyond our control, such as experiencing overwhelming feelings or watching our alcoholic loved ones face the consequences of their actions, many of us almost automatically look for someone to blame or resent. Some of us spend hours cataloguing injustices and having endless conversations with people who aren't there. Or we turn on ourselves, attacking with such weapons as shame, guilt, self-hatred, and doubt.

We might behave self-destructively or even contemplate suicide. Our thoughts lead us to believe that we are not good enough, that our circumstances aren't good enough, that we don't have enough and don't do enough, and that we are victims, without reason to hope. Even after years of recovery, we may badger ourselves: "After ___ years in Al-Anon, I shouldn't be in this situation" or "A spiritual person wouldn't feel this way."

Like any feelings, unless we let them surface, they can dominate us. We may still need to feel blame, regret, doubt, and resentment, without censorship, before we can set them aside. It can be extremely helpful to acknowledge and share these thoughts with an Al-Anon Sponsor or other members of the fellowship. Once these thoughts and feelings come out into the light, we have something to work with.

In the long run, however, many of us have found that whether the finger points at us or at someone else, whenever we attack, we lose. Either we entrench ourselves more firmly in the belief that we are helpless victims in a hostile world or we teach ourselves that we really do deserve abuse. Negative thoughts can divert our attention from working on ourselves, our true feelings, and our responsibilities. In time, these thoughts can be as destructive for us as alcohol is for the alcoholic.

Some of us really have been victimized in the past. We may have had few choices then; or we may not have recognized the choices that were available to us. Today we know the choice is in our hands—*we* decide whether or not to remain victims. In Al-Anon we learn that changed attitudes can aid recovery. What we teach ourselves with our thoughts and attitudes is up to us.

Reflections on Responsibility and Detachment

Choosing Not to Enable

The other day my husband and I had to face our alcoholic son and tell him that we could no longer enable him to continue as he was. He had lost another job, his wife was taking their new baby to her parent's home in another state, and yet he was not any closer to reaching for help. This time he would have to help himself.

Probably the hardest thing I have ever done was turn away from this young person to whom I gave life. To see the sad, lost look in his beautiful eyes and the sag of his broad shoulders, to stand by and watch him walk away with that slow, shuffling gait was like tearing out a part of me. We realized that the help we were giving him was actually only giving him the means to continue his addiction. I said, "Thy will be done, God," even though I knew in my heart I did not necessarily want His will done. I wanted my son back, healthy and strong.

Al-Anon's First Step reminds me that regardless of what I want or don't want, I am powerless over my son. If I must turn him loose to hold him, then with God's help and the support from Al-Anon, I can "Let Go and Let God." I can learn to detach with love without feeling that I am deserting him.

Powerless Over Others' Pain

"It's something you read about in the papers." Those were my words over and over again after I learned my daughter had been incestuously involved with and blackmailed by her alcoholic stepfather. It's difficult to find anything to be grateful for when a situation like that happens. My Al-Anon Sponsor encouraged me to try. It wasn't long before I found myself being grateful that my daughter could speak up and let us know what was going on, that she wasn't pregnant, that there was no other physical damage, and that she was alive. Other parents haven't always been so lucky. I found myself consumed by hate for the man who had done this. I knew only one sure release and it was a tough way to go. I started praying for him. My first prayers were, "God, please bless that b—d." Eventually I could say his name and with time my Higher Power gave me release.

I wanted to take the pain from my daughter and have it myself, but in Al-Anon I learned I was powerless over her pain. As my Higher Power restored me to sanity, I realized all I could do was to be there and to reassure her that she didn't do anything wrong. Al-Anon members reminded me to take care of myself, so I could be there for her. Bless my Higher Power for directing us to a wonderful counselor with compassion, understanding, and humor—a fine gift at such a time.

My daughter is coming along fine. I feel she will always have the scars, but I have learned to trust that her Higher Power is working in her life and I must leave to Him what is His to do.

Tools for Detachment

My husband and I did not find a pink cloud when we first got into AA and Al-Anon; we didn't have the honeymoon phase that many seem to have. The first two years of sobriety were worse than anything we had during the active drinking. I was in a state of confusion, and did not yet have a handle on the Al-Anon principles that would prevent my being devastated by his behavior. He was, for the first and only time in our marriage, verbally abusive beyond belief.

I was first reminded that for the alcoholic, drinking is not the problem—it's the solution. Alcohol had served as the source of his security, courage, and serenity. Today he is often in a state of panic because he has not yet found other sources for these very real needs.

Al-Anon does not promise to save marriages, but it does offer sanity. If you do want the marriage, they told me, then accept the fact that you will not get healthy behavior from a sick person or logical statements from an illogical person. This includes me, too. I expected myself to be well immediately. Now I know that I may never be, but that I can be increasingly better, and I can be gentler with both of us.

I was also reminded that we do not accept the unacceptable, and what is unacceptable varies from person to person. What I could not live with for five minutes, others could perhaps tolerate with good grace, and vice versa.

They said to look at the possibility that I might be accepting sick behavior. Do I seek out suffering and abuse? I looked hard at this one before I decided it really was not true in my case.

I was especially warned not to walk on eggshells for fear of arousing his wrath during that time. I was told that an alcoholic controls his family by drinking: "Don't do that or Daddy might get drunk." It is small improvement when he begins to control by anger: "Don't do that or Daddy might get mad." I learned that as long as I acted with love and courtesy, his anger was his problem.

All of this was useful, but I needed specific, concrete, how-to-do-it suggestions. Members of my group shared these three ideas that really got me through those months:

1. Build an invisible shield between you and him, a shield of love. Use it when the abuse begins, and the words will hit it and roll off without touching you. Visualize it keenly; make it vividly real in your mind.

2. Remember that he is only one or two years old in AA, that he is much like a real baby of that age who slaps out at people who are holding him. We don't slap back. We just hold the baby off far enough that he can't hit us.

3. When he is holding forth with these torrents of vicious words, they told me, picture him saying these things out the window of a mental hospital. Would they hurt then? No, I thought, because I would know he was sick and that they weren't aimed at me personally. Members suggested that I mentally draw a window around him whenever this started and detach myself as if he were really hospitalized. It worked amazingly! I can't

tell you how many hundreds of times I drew the window around him and felt the release that came as a result.

I would not have lived that way indefinitely. Some people do not change; my husband did. It was a phase of his recovery, as there have been other painful phases, and they passed. His sponsor kept saying, "It is impossible to attend meetings regularly and never change. Either you will change or you will get so uncomfortable you will quit attending meetings." We did change.

Learning to Love and Trust Again

I moved in with my alcoholic father four years ago; I was being sexually abused by my stepfather and saw this geographical change as my only escape—I couldn't speak up, but I did get out. I initially applied Alateen only to my life in an alcoholic situation. I have since learned to use the program in dealing with the experience of being molested.

One of the tools is the Serenity Prayer—accepting what I cannot change and changing what I can. I had to accept the pain of facing what I had been through and then learn all I could about the sexual abuse of children. Alateen helps me to understand that my stepfather is sick, like the alcoholic. I didn't cause his behavior. Still, I am hurt that no one stopped him.

Because I went through so much alone, I have a hard time believing that anyone cares about me. I am just now learning to accept love from other people. I remember various scenes very vividly and have to deal with that pain.

But I also want to put the experience in the past and go on. This means being very honest with myself and using the Fourth Step to uncover character traits that resulted from being abused. For instance, I know that I am a people-pleaser, so anxious to do anything to feel loved that I don't always take very good care of myself.

As a child, I was a victim; now, it is my responsibility to learn to love and trust again. In looking at myself, I also appreciate that I am stronger and more understanding because of my experience.

My Obligation to Be Myself

During the drinking years I played "Let's pretend" so diligently and convincingly that I myself believed we were a "normal" family and something as un-nice as alcoholism just couldn't happen to us. I went into Al-Anon reluctantly. For years I continued to handle all my tumultuous feelings with food. I talked about the program but not about me; I told people what I thought, not how I felt. I didn't know how I felt!

At meeting after meeting, Al-Anon members suggested that I would not recover unless I dropped the phoniness and learned to relate genuinely with my whole self. I believed this and told other people the same thing: "Be yourself. The reaction of other people is their choice!" But in actual fact, I was not always willing to pay the emotional price of being myself, particularly with my husband. He couldn't handle my depression, my anger, my bitchiness. He depended on my total "okay-ness"—and why not? For many years I had carefully seen to it that all he had to relate to was that facade.

Al-Anon taught me that enabling can take many forms. When I protect my husband from having to cope with the real me, I keep him from having the chance to grow and change, just as I protected him from the consequences of his drinking. I am not truly loving him if I deny him this opportunity for growth.

Nor am I being loving to me. If I am not my true self around others then I don't grow. I'll have no identity. I won't know who I am because I haven't taken the time to know myself. I cannot encapsulate one area of my life—it "leaks" into all the other areas, like a sock in the wash. I cannot say, "I will be myself here," and "I will be someone else there," without losing touch with who I am.

I will always feel safer with some people than with others. I will feel vulnerable and somewhat scared when I express my true self for the first time—or the first one hundred! I cannot let down my guard all the time with everybody. Sometimes the emotional price truly *is* more than I can pay. In Al-Anon I was told not to go to the hardware store for milk—I don't share my innermost dreams with someone who will scoff at them. I have a right to privacy and a right to protect myself. Relating on a feeling level doesn't mean that I become an emotional exhibitionist with no regard for what is appropriate in a given set of circumstances. It does mean that, although I cannot relate to everyone on a deep, meaningful level, I can let you know my true feelings, even if we just discuss the weather.

Getting Even or Getting Better

I was the last person on earth capable of infidelity. It was something my neighbors, coworkers, or people on television did. I took my wedding vows seriously and to the letter. When I found out my husband was having an affair, I was so angry that I hit him so hard he needed stitches. This gave him the impetus to leave and move in with her. I even helped him pack.

The hurt was so incredibly big. I was devastated. He was gone less than a week and I was looking for an affair. If my husband could do it, so could I. I decided to "show him" and immediately got involved with a mutual friend of ours. I remember how wonderful it felt just to be hugged and held by someone who seemed to care, even if it was just for the moment. I also remember the shame I felt at getting involved with a married man. Now I was just as guilty as my husband's newfound lady friend. I discouraged future "rematches" by avoiding my friend for the next year. (Eventually, with the help of my Sponsor, I was able to face him. I told him I had made a terrible mistake that I did not wish to repeat, and that I valued him as a friend.)

I felt so worthless with my husband gone that I could think of no reason to go on living. My life felt "over" and I was not even 30 years old. I wanted to kill the pain, so I went to bars and picked up guys for one-night stands. I didn't want responsibilities—just to know I was loveable and attractive, even if I wasn't to my husband. I hated what I had become; in fact, I was appalled at my own behavior.

When an AA friend of mine told me that the reason
my husband had taken up with another woman was not
because I was bad in bed, I was stunned. What I couldn't
hear him say was that alcoholism is a disease that affects
people's values. My husband's actions had nothing to do
with me. The messages finally got through to me after I
broke down and went to Al-Anon. Pretty soon, I found
that I was getting more relief from Al-Anon than I was
from the one-night stands. When I stopped this behavior, I began feeling better about myself. Before long I
was going out to coffee after meetings, and learning
to feel loved and accepted by my newfound Al-Anon
friends. I realized that I could have continued to have
affairs with men, but it wouldn't ease my pain or bring
my husband back. And maybe I didn't really want him
back.

By learning to love myself and to become my own
friend, as well as a friend to others in the program, my
self-destructiveness and self-hatred stopped. I recognized
I was nowhere near ready to have relationships with
men. I needed to get resolved with myself and with my
marriage. I had to take responsibility for my choices, no
matter what my husband did. Al-Anon turned my life
around very quickly. I am very grateful to my Higher
Power for bringing me into the program when I needed
it most. I realize now that it took something drastic like
infidelity to "shock me" into Al-Anon. There were a lot
of hard lessons that came faster than I would have liked,
but Al-Anon saved my life. Having affairs and directing
my focus at getting back at my husband are no longer

options. Now I am practicing these principles in every area of my life.

No Longer Blaming Myself

When violence first occurred in my marriage, I truly thought it was my fault and that I should never say or do anything to anger my alcoholic husband. If I did, I thought he was justified, because in my mind he was always right; therefore I must be wrong. Because I didn't want to think badly of him, I just denied that any violence occurred. However, it was violence that brought me to Al-Anon, where I learned I was dealing with a very sick person, and that I, too, was ill. I often needed to be reminded that I didn't cause the disease of alcoholism, I can't control it, and I can't cure it. I no longer have to blame myself for another person's actions. By focusing on myself and working my program without all that blame, I can recover from the effects of this disease. Al-Anon has literally saved my life.

Understanding Detachment

I am presently living with a sober alcoholic, which at times feels like sitting on a time bomb that could explode at any minute. I have been in Alateen for a few years and still find detachment the hardest thing to understand. Finally I realized that detachment is not caring less, it's caring more for my own serenity.

Detachment or Denial

When my older sister told me she had been molested

by my father when she was very young, I felt frightened, ashamed, and angry with her. I don't like reporting this reaction, but I hope that doing so may help me to move on. At first I tried to just turn it over—to picture my sister, my father, and myself in God's hands—and to detach myself. Perhaps I was trying to ignore or deny what I had heard. At the same time I felt responsible, as though I could have somehow exercised control over events that occurred before my conception.

I was helped by another Al-Anon member who had also felt guilty about incest between his father and sisters. I came to recognize the same feeling that I had about other facets of the cunning, baffling, and powerful disease of alcoholism: the feeling that I am to blame. I guess I'd rather blame myself than feel the grief of the devastation of living with this disease.

I was overwhelmed—depressed, frustrated, and angry. I heard someone at a meeting say that when he had recently felt depressed, his Sponsor had reminded him that "It's just alcoholism." It wasn't complicated; he didn't need to figure it out. He was experiencing one of the effects of the disease. This helped me.

I told my Sponsor I was considering getting professional help to sort out my feelings, and he supported me in this choice. One of the key elements of my recovery in Al-Anon has been to become willing to seek and accept help with problems, not just within the fellowship but from other sources as well.

As I worked on my feelings about my sister's report of incest, I came to understand and accept her heightened sense of physical danger in the world. I could even accept more fully that my childhood had also had its very scary moments. More difficult to admit is that I came to realize I don't have an open mind about her report. I'm not proud of this, but I do feel some relief to know where I stand. Things take time; more will be revealed. I need to keep in mind that I don't have to accept her experience as my experience. I only have to accept her experience as hers.

In the meantime, I am thankful for the trust my sister demonstrated in telling me her story, and I am thankful for the deeper sense of understanding that I feel when I deal with her.

Asking for What I Need

I asked anonymously at an Al-Anon meeting how to deal with my husband's inability to give affection. Well, in Al-Anon we get what we need, which isn't always what we ask for. I was told that it is unrealistic and unfair to expect all my affection to come from one person. This is especially true if that person is an alcoholic. I realized I expected my spouse to read my mind, to know when I wanted affection, how I wanted it, and how much I wanted.

Today it is still not easy for me to express my need for affection. However, I have widened my circle of affection, which has taken the pressure off my spouse. Affection and attention received do not measure how lovable a person I am. I can determine that. As I recognize my character defects and assets I am slowly realizing that I am a good person.

Detaching by Focusing on Myself

I was heartsick to know my worst suspicions had been accurate when I learned of my husband's infidelity, but that heartsickness was outweighed by the relief of knowing I was not crazy. I asked him to please live elsewhere. My sense of self-worth returned at once. In what I considered to be practicing Al-Anon in its best sense, I was taking care of me. My Al-Anon friends gave me the support I needed to remain true to my convictions.

Miracles do happen. My husband went into treatment for alcoholism and eventually convinced the therapists as well as me that he was sincere about wanting to make a serious commitment to our marriage, including being a faithful husband. So, with hope and apprehension, we reconciled. I was as surprised as anyone.

I believe I played a part in his decision by not interfering. I detached—and with love. By separating, I saved myself the agony of wondering what he was doing and with whom. By default I followed Al-Anon's experience—minding my own business.

Sometimes during these past months I've questioned my feelings: Am I too sensitive or is "it" happening again? I don't want to dwell upon my fear and turn it into a self-fulfilling prophecy. I'm giving myself as much time for the trust to return as it took to lose it—"One Day at a Time."

Detaching with Love

After several years of increasing drinking, my wife had finally given up the struggle. Having spent weeks draining countless bottles of vodka and not eating, she wound up in the hospital in a coma from which she was not expected to recover. I had lost any desire to help her. Nothing I had done seemed to make any difference. I became totally indifferent; if she died, at least I could get back to a normal, orderly life. Where Al-Anon told me to detach with love, I detached with ruthless efficiency and total unconcern.

I would sit by her bed, hold her hand, and talk to her, though of course there was no response. Al-Anon and AA members whom we knew (and many we didn't) seemed always to be there. They prayed for her—and for me.

One day I had an experience that changed my life. It was summer, and my wife's feet were uncovered. I noticed that her toenails were long, curling, and ugly. I finally realized how she had neglected herself. Though she had once been a pretty girl who was always well-dressed, the drinking years had created an awesome change. For the first time I was able to separate the disease of alcoholism from the wonderful woman I remembered. Like a flood, all my love for her came rushing back. All the good years and the happiness she had once given me came back to me. I suppose I had deliberately shut them out of my mind. Here was my darling wife whose endless struggle against the terrible disease I had done nothing to support. Al-Anon told me to detach from the disease, not from the person. What right had I to be so indifferent?

I sat by her and prayed to a God I did not accept. Was it imagination that suggested some reaction in the hand I was holding? A few days later there was a clear response in her grip, and soon after she opened her eyes. While she will never be entirely recovered, she is back at home now, able to look after herself during the day. She is now simply the most precious thing in my life. I am no longer the same person. The spirit that had been dead so long in me has reawakened.

Letting Go of Guilt and Shame

I was raised in a very violent, alcoholic home. My family denies it or just doesn't want to talk about it. But there wasn't a day that someone didn't get hit or thrown against a wall. Today I'm 32 years old and have a daughter, eight, and a son, two-years old. I beat my daughter for the first seven years of her life, and did the same to my son during his first year, until I joined Al-Anon.

One day I realized that I had to turn over my shame and guilt to my Higher Power, as these were the two major roadblocks preventing me from growing in this program. I had caused a lot of pain for my children, the one thing I always swore I'd never do to my kids when I grew up. I hated myself so much and wanted to die for all those awful things I did to them. Finally I had to " Let Go and Let God" take care of me and my children.

Getting My Focus Back

My husband, a recovering alcoholic, finally got me

into Al-Anon 21 years ago after asking me to go many times. I loved it and have been going ever since.

Several years ago we started taking care of an epileptic widow. We took her to church, to places where we went, even to family gatherings. She couldn't and wouldn't go anywhere unless we took her. When we had other things to do, she tried to make us feel guilty. I thought I knew all about focusing on myself after all my years in Al-Anon. But I lost touch with my program and became so upset that I could only think and talk about her and her problems. Poor me, how I had to put up with her and all of her accusations.

One evening at Al-Anon I realized I was back in my pre-Al-Anon days! She was controlling me! I was forgetting everything I had learned. I needed to hear, "No one can hurt you unless you let them." Getting my focus back wasn't easy. It was murder! I even started having fainting spells. I ended up consulting a neurologist before I finally heard what I needed to hear at one good Al-Anon meeting.

I never thought it could happen to me. I was sure I knew all the answers and only needed to encourage others. Now I know I must work this beautiful program every day.

Changing My Attitudes
When I met my husband at a dance just after the Second World War, he had had too much to drink, but I didn't really notice. I was enchanted by this good-looking young man who knew how to treat a lady and was a

fantastic dancer.

About six months after we met he was in court on his first drunk driving charge. I felt so ashamed that I even went to see the editor of our local newspaper to keep it out of the papers. Only later did I realize how obvious it was to others that I was trying desperately to change this man.

Eventually physical violence developed, and, looking back, I see that I often provoked it. Our second daughter was born some weeks early due to my tussling with my husband at the top of the stairs. I think I was trying to get him to go to bed; anyway, I lost my balance and tumbled down the stairs. The baby was born soon after. My husband arrived with a huge bouquet and charmed all the nurses. They thought my tears were post-natal blues because I could not divulge my despair and my fears for the future.

This sort of thing continued for years, and then a miracle seemed to take place. My husband attended AA and saw a psychiatrist, and I found the help and support I needed in Al-Anon. For the first time since I married, I had friends. Thank goodness I did, for when my husband suffered a relapse after ten months sobriety, I was devastated. I ran tearfully to a phone to call my Sponsor. Then I made the first of many train trips to her home. We had many calming chats and shared a whole lot of common sense. She told me to stop feeling sorry for myself. Later I thought, "Rotten bitch, she says I'm only feeling sorry for myself." (Which I was.)

"Keep busy," my Al-Anon group suggested. I made

sure I ate well and got enough sleep. I learned to leave some housework to do in the evening. I took out my anger and resentment as I polished the floor of our living room. Our floor really shone. When I complained that the rooms needed redecorating and my husband would not do anything, it was suggested that I might make a start on the work and remind myself that I was doing it for me, because I wanted it to look nice.

The children learned not to rely on their father's promises and I learned not to make promises at all. One day at an Al-Anon meeting I heard someone say that the calm attitude she had learned to adopt seemed to have a positive effect on her children and her alcoholic husband. I vowed to try this. I stopped shouting at the children, and they stopped shouting at each other. I spoke quietly to my husband and learned to ignore his goading remarks; it even became amusing and I had to try not to laugh. My sense of humor began to come back.

I had never been a churchgoer and was inclined to say that God never listened to me because my prayers were usually something like this: "Please God, don't let him get drunk tonight." I discovered that I had to listen to God.

My husband is really a kind and caring man at heart, and over the years we have both mellowed a great deal. Today he knows that I truly love him, even though I hate what drinking can do to him.

Not Responsible for Another's Actions

I was a victim of child molesting long before I can remember. My sister told me she beat a male member of my family off of me with a broom when I was three years old—and it only got worse. I was terrified to tell anyone because I was threatened every time. I grew up feeling very bad and very responsible for all this. The guilt I bore certainly had an effect on the decisions I made in my life.

I had a beautiful daughter, and I swore this would never happen to her. It did, and again I felt the horrible guilt, both for her and for me. I left the man, but too late.

Today, through the grace of God, I have several years of Al-Anon recovery. I learned through my Fourth Step that I wasn't and am not responsible for someone else's actions. Unfortunately, my daughter hasn't been so lucky. She turned to drugs and alcohol and doesn't—or can't—deal with the effects of sexual abuse on her life. She has been in jail, and once almost died of an overdose. From the depths of my soul, I pray that my beautiful daughter may be healed of her deep scars. All I can do at this point is to love her and put her in God's care. I don't have the answers, but through searching, looking, praying, and following the Al-Anon program, I have a good life with some peace of mind and soul.

Detaching with the Help of My Higher Power

With violence entering the family situation, my daughter walked to the nearby hospital and told the emergency staff that if she did not get help immediately she would probably take her life. At the same time my husband was fired from his job. During all of this, I held on to Al-Anon for dear life. It seemed when things couldn't get worse, they always did. But my Higher Power carried me when I couldn't walk. Countless times I cried to Him to keep me from falling apart.

My daughter decided that life in our house was too demanding. We still do not know where she is, who she is with, or whether her efforts to make it on her own will succeed. Detaching from her is many times harder than detaching from my husband, and right now I am counting on my Higher Power to see me through this crisis. I know there is a reason for everything, and I must keep an open mind to find out what it is. I have to work very hard on not projecting about what might happen and trust in His will. Her Higher Power will take care of her, and I must try to take care of myself with His help.

The problems created by alcoholism in my life are so far-reaching—but not insurmountable. The foundation I have developed in Al-Anon not only makes me grateful when things are going good, but also makes me realize that the program works especially when things go badly. There are no guarantees that life will turn out the way we would like, but the program has shown me God's will is the only way; it is up to me to work with Him and turn my life and will over to His care and guidance.

Taking Responsibility for Myself
Covering up or lying about abuse is taking on some-

one else's responsibility. In my alcoholic household, I covered up my mother's abuse and never told my father or anyone. I protected her and did not allow natural consequences to take their course. My children did the same for me: they protected me from the knowledge of what was going on and resented me for not taking care of them. In Al-Anon I have learned that I cannot expect anyone to help me unless I am willing to share that I *need* help.

Accepting Others' Choices

Being in Al-Anon has helped me to step back and look at problems with a minimum of emotion involved—to detach. I figure it took my son 14 years to arrive in jail. All the choices along the line were his. Somewhere within him are the teachings he heard while in treatment and AA meetings, and one day they may surface. In the meantime, I have turned my concerns about my son over to God. The strength I derive from the Al-Anon program and my faith are letting me go about my business cheerfully. That's my choice. My son's choices are his.

Removing Myself from Battles

No matter what, no one has the right to physically abuse anyone. I had to separate my own behavior from the abuser's behavior before I could realize that the abuse was his problem, not mine. I did this by removing myself from the battles, sometimes just emotionally. Arguments are useless against sickness, and in this case, abuse is a symptom of the disease of alcoholism. Talking to a person who is in a rage is a waste of time. I'm better off talking to my Al-Anon Sponsor instead. I am taking the unnecessary risk of being hurt when I meet anger with anger.

The Effects of Alcoholism

My husband never was very interested in sex. I thought he had lost interest in sex during his previous marriage. I was going to make everything okay. When I couldn't, I felt like a failure. I thought I wasn't sexy enough. Later, when he left me and became involved with a prostitute, I felt there was really something wrong with me. Thanks to Al-Anon, I learned that his actions had nothing to do with me, but instead reflected the progression of his alcoholism. That was hard for me to accept, but I realized that without Al-Anon, we were all spiraling downward.

I feel that I saved myself and my children with God's help through Al-Anon and the people who love me. Though my husband eventually committed suicide, I believe that he loved us as much as he was able.

It has been a rough road to recovery, but I know I'm on the right track. Hopefully, when I'm ready, my Higher Power will see fit for me to have another relationship—one that is healthy, stable, and committed.

Accepting My Powerlessness

For the second time within a year, my husband moved out for no apparent reason. When I went to the place where he was staying, I found him with someone else. I was angry, I was hurt, and I was numb. My stomach ached and I felt sick inside. I wanted to tear him apart piece by piece. Instead, sick as I was, I sat down, talked to both of them calmly, and said it was okay. The end result was that my husband didn't have to face up to what he had done to me and to our marriage. The truth was it really wasn't okay. I felt as if I would go crazy.

With the help of open AA meetings, I began to understand my husband's actions. With the help of Al-Anon, I came to terms with myself and was able to accept alcoholism as a disease that changes people—a disease over which we have no control. Through Al-Anon I learned to give my life to God, to live my life, and let my husband live his. I learned not to argue, not to condemn, nor enable, but to be patient and let God handle my day. Most of all, I learned kindness and compassion towards my husband. With this, each day there is less hurt, less resentment, and more honest forgiveness and love. Al-Anon has given me hope, patience, and—yes—peace inside myself.

Helping or Enabling

A phone call one day left me feeling as if there had been a death in the family. An AA member had called to say that our son had decided to commit himself to treatment for alcohol addiction. Oh, yes, we knew he drank. There were many signs of a problem. They had been there for years. Yes, we had even talked about it. He had a problem. We should do something about it.

And we did something. Every morning we yelled to wake him up so that he would be on time for school and, later, for work. If he didn't feel like going to school, it was easier to let him stay home and write a note. Later we would "loan" him small amounts of money, "to help him out." I walked on eggs because I did not want to upset him.

After the phone call, my world was in shambles. Why was it easier to accept a drinking son than one who was trying to stay sober? The same AA member led me to Al-Anon, where I learned that my kind of help over the years was really harming the alcoholic by helping him to drink. I had tried to take over his responsibilities. I had to learn to take care of myself and detach, with love, from the alcoholic.

Detaching from My Fear

The financial decline in our marriage was as insidious as the alcoholism. The signs were there all along, yet it happened so gradually that when the crunch came, it seemed as if the roof had crashed in all at once. A car we had bought was repossessed and we almost lost our home. The good news was that my alcoholic husband reached his own bottom and found sobriety.

Just as alcoholism is progressive, so is recovery from its effects. It took ten years to pay off all the old debts. I remember the early days when we took turns going to our respective Al-Anon and AA meetings because we couldn't afford a babysitter.

Financially, things did get much better in time. We

even decided to buy a new house. But during this period I developed terrible fears of financial disaster. I imagined every scenario possible in which tragedy would strike. It was an old house—what if something major went wrong? It was near a river—what if there was a flood? What if we had sickness, medical bills, death...? I told my self-induced horror story to anyone in Al-Anon who would listen. Invariable, when I sought magic and a sure-fire guarantee, I was given the soothing reassurance that the only magic answer was to try to take it one day at a time. For today, I did have a roof over my head and food on the table. Slowly but surely the panic lessened. The recurring nightmare of seeing myself and my family and our furniture out on the curb subsided. The process began by taking another searching inventory and facing the exact nature of my fears. I found that I equated financial security with self-worth. As with every other difficulty I have encountered since I came into Al-Anon, a daily turning over of my will to the God of my understanding and a realization that I could find solace through improving my conscious contact with this God ultimately provided the true healing.

Allowing Others to Be Responsible for Themselves

One of the effects of alcoholism has been that I have been overly involved in other people's choices. If I feel responsible for someone else's behavior, then I have not detached from whatever I am allowing to embarrass, frustrate, or otherwise bother me. I am still thinking of that person as belonging to me, as a possession rather than an individual. I used to lay out my loved one's clothes, so that his appearance would represent me well. In Al-Anon I learned that by doing this I am really insinuating that he is less capable than I am of selecting what he wishes to wear. I objected, saying, "But I like to lay out his clothes for him, and he likes it too." Of course I did—it let me pretend that I had control.

Setting Limits

I came into Al-Anon because I'd fallen in love with an active alcoholic. As the layers of the onion peeled away, however, I had to address the issue of abuse in all my relationships, past and present. It is not my business to define any of my family members as alcoholic. I can, however, have feelings about behaviors and attitudes, and I can recognize where I have repeated old family patterns.

I realized that, like my mother, I had enabled one sister who found no time to care for her children. When they acted out in their teens, people came to me, not my sister. Now, 20 years later, I was still playing caretaker, protecting others from my sister's increasingly abusive behavior. For example, when my mother would calmly tell me how my sister took advantage of her, I would get angry for her and argue with my sister to stop that behavior.

When I finally focused on myself and stopped fighting my mother's battles, I told my sister that her behavior was unacceptable and abusive to *me*. She had no idea what I meant and made no attempt to change her behavior. Finally, I refused to go home for the holidays. My mother was very upset. "But it's only for one day!" she protested. Although my choice saved me from another spoiled holiday, I felt a great sense of loss because of my mother's inability to come to my aid. It was a pattern I remembered well from childhood.

Three years later, I still don't visit very often and am considered the aberrant child. I miss the old feeling of closeness with my mother, although I realize it was based on a lack of boundaries. There is a bittersweet quality about my newfound independence and good mental health. I love my new life and new friends in Al-Anon. They are caring and supportive and revel with me in my new accomplishments. It is sad that my mother is threatened by these same accomplishments and feels she has lost me in some way. There is no Utopia where I never have to feel pain or sadness again—Al-Anon never promised me that. It did offer me a life with some serenity, regardless of what was going on around me, if on a daily basis I used the principles the program had to offer. I find this as I continue the commitment to practice these principles one day at a time.

Healing Anger and Blame

The bomb hit after my husband had been in AA and I had been in Al-Anon for many years: my daughter told me that, before sobriety, her father had used her in a sexual encounter. I was in shock. I wanted to punish him, but he was a different person now. He had made amends to my daughter sometime before, and she was receiving professional help. The past was over, and the person he had really harmed had forgiven him.

However, my guilt said, "If you had been a better mother, you would have been more alert and would have divorced him. Then she would never have had to endure such a traumatic experience." Self-hatred raged in me: "How could you be so sick, choosing a man like that!" Violent, bitter hatred for him consumed me. I tried to pray, telling God I wanted to turn my life and will over to Him and learn forgiveness, but I knew I was lying. I realized that I didn't really believe God would or could do anything about this mire into which our family seemed to be sinking. That's when I started over and went back to the basic principles I had learned as an Al-Anon beginner. I am very grateful I told my Sponsor about all this because I needed to talk about it daily for a long time. I read and re-read Al-Anon literature, went to extra meetings, and put a great deal of energy into the Steps. I also saw a counselor. I was told, "What you feed will grow." I decided to feed my health and right thinking instead of my anger, pride, fear, and guilt.

Roses do not bloom overnight. We have struggled at times, but as we have persistently worked on ourselves and our commitment to each other, much healing has taken place. I pray each day that God will be in the center of every relationship I have. The first time I prayed this because I wanted my husband to change. What has happened is that I have changed and I see God in me. I have learned to trust again and to live more in reality than ever. I know what a miracle is.

CHAPTER FIVE

Surrender

"Let Go and Let God." It sounds so simple. But when our circumstances or the circumstances of those we love weigh heavily on our minds, we may have no idea how to do it. Some of us struggle with the very idea of a Higher Power. Others begin to question long and deeply held beliefs, especially in stressful times.

We may grow impatient with ourselves, certain that there must be a way to avoid all this strife and that we must be doing something wrong. Many of us review the same scenario again and again, looking for that elusive answer that will solve everything. We obsessively wrack our brains for something different that we could do or should have done. At the same time, we wish we could just quit fighting ourselves. As long as there is a chance of figuring out a solution, we reason, we should keep trying—even if days or months of such efforts have led to nothing but frustration and an increasing sense of desperation and urgency. We may secretly feel that this problem is too important to trust to God, as if we had the power to prevent God's will from unfolding by the mere exercise of our resistance. We fear that if we surrender, anything could happen—our worst nightmares could come true.

In a way that is true: anything could happen. Even something wonderful.

Actually, anything could happen whether we let go or not. It is an illusion that as long as we cling to the situation we have some control and can prevent distressing outcomes from touching our lives. Surrender means accepting our powerlessness to change many of the realities of our lives, even when we find those realities to be devastating. It means trusting instead in a Power greater than ourselves. Faith has been likened to being in a dark tunnel and seeing no glimmer of light, but still crawling forward as if we did. Though our circumstances may seem dark indeed, when we turn to a Higher Power rather than to our own stubborn wills, we have already begun to move toward the light.

Reflections on Surrender

Becoming Willing to Surrender

I try to think how I became willing to admit I was powerless over alcohol and others. I feel that, in my great pain, God opened my mind to what Al-Anon members were saying about doing something different. If you normally met the alcoholic at the door saying, "You have been out all night," or if you stayed awake all night, you worked on changing these habits. I treated myself to a nice bubble bath, laid out my prettiest nightgown, and got ready for a good night. If, however, I still could not sleep, I reached for that good old Al-Anon Conference Approved Literature and read and read. (God gave me a lot of time to read because He knew I needed it so very much.)

Now came the hard part. Believing that God could work miracles in my life was one thing; being willing to step aside and let Him do His work was something else. When the pain became so great that I thought I could not bear it anymore, I said to God, "I would like this person in my life, but if you have other plans, it's okay. I will accept what you have for me." After this, little by little, changes started taking place in my life. I would take the time to think before I said silly things like, "If you loved me you wouldn't drink," or "Don't you know that you are killing yourself with that stuff?" I found I had a full-time job just working on myself.

Letting Go and Letting God

When my daughter left alcoholism treatment and went back to school, where she had attempted suicide, I had to let go. I reached out to my Al-Anon friends and my program and I read my *One Day at a Time in Al-Anon* book. I used all the tools the program offers, especially my telephone list. But I used the Eleventh Step the most. It is a wonderful Step because it says we can find "knowledge of His will for us and the power to carry that out." It doesn't say, "Show me Your will and let me struggle on my own." It tells me that God is there and He will give me the help I need.

It was very hard not to be overly protective. I wanted to tell everyone, "You can't do this to my daughter because she's special, she's fragile, she's vulnerable." I wanted to take her pain away, even though I had my own pain. I had to learn to let her be her own person.

Five years later, when she went through a similar alcoholic cycle, *she* caught herself, recognized the depression, and went into an alcohol treatment program. It was a good reminder that my daughter has her own path and her own Higher Power. My job is to work on *my* recovery.

Ready to Give Up the Struggle

Am I willing to give up the pain of trying to control my partner? Am I willing to give up my silent contempt, scornful looks, and disapproving comments, no matter how justified I think I am? Am I willing to admit that I am powerless over him as well as my own emotional reactions? Am I willing to admit that my life is unmanageable when I react in this way?

Yes! I am tired of fighting. I am weary of analyzing the relationship and each interaction. This scrutiny began long before my husband found sobriety, long before I found Al-Anon, and has continued well into recovery. Enough! I turn to my Higher Power for the serenity, courage, and acceptance I need to let go of my control and let God take over, to live my own life, and let my husband live his.

My experience in Al-Anon assures me that God will do for me what I cannot do alone. I don't have to understand it. Trying to understand only locks me up inside my head.

Finding Release from Obsession

Right after I joined Al-Anon, my second marriage broke up. It was shocking to discover my low self-esteem, my inability to communicate honestly, and my incredibly overpowering need for a man in my life. Within three weeks of breaking up with my alcoholic husband I was seeing another man. After a time he told me that he could not handle my suffocating emotional attachment, and we stopped seeing each other. Within one week there was another man in my life—and then another. I resolved to get better on my own, without a man.

Soon afterward, I was introduced to my brother's

closest military buddy. As time went by, I became emotionally attached again, then dependent, then totally obsessed, as if addicted to him. I knew I was out of control. My outrageous behavior continued until one day his letter informed me that he would no longer tolerate this suffocation.

I had prayed for release from my obsession and received it, but ending the relationship wasn't what I'd had in mind. Overwhelming pain of rejection and abandonment totally engulfed me. For days the sobbing and screams of anger went on and on. Al-Anon meetings saved my sanity. Members of the fellowship suggested a connection between alcoholism and my desperate behavior. In looking for the source of my security and wholeness outside myself, I had been going to the hardware store for bread. I learned that I could be whole in my relationship to my Higher Power, that I was all right. During this time I was forced to depend on my Higher Power totally and completely.

Ever so slowly this special man returned, cautiously and carefully. In time I discovered I was no longer the obsessed person I once had been. In Al-Anon I was becoming a more confident woman with trust in a Higher Power who loves me, cares for me, accepts me, and forgives me unconditionally.

Through this dark time in my life I learned to live in a more balanced way—to share and care for another human being while giving him the freedom to develop in his own way. My relationship with this man is strong and healthy today because I am supported by God's love.

Love and Surrender

I have replaced the day-to-day pain and guilt I experienced while my son sank into the world of alcohol, drugs, suicide attempts, crime, and finally prison, by letting go in Al-Anon. Looking back, it seems as if it all happened to someone else. When my son came home from prison, the atmosphere in our home had deteriorated into an ugly black silence between his parents.

An alcoholic daughter and her baby were back with us. My son could never stand her for very long. She cried a lot. He raged a lot. I cried a lot. One day as they yelled at one another more and more savagely, I threw up my hands in despair and said, "I give up. I give up. I cannot make anyone in my family love one another, and I need help!"

It was the greatest moment of my life, and I went to my first Al-Anon meeting a couple days later. It was never easy but it was always better after that. My tools were willingness to listen and change, no matter how long it took, no matter how great the pain. It could get better, they said, and it did, hour-by-hour, day-by-day.

In letting go with love and—with the help of the Al-Anon program—seeing to my own recovery, my son has finally found recovery in AA, at least for today. Tomorrow, who knows? That's his tomorrow, not mine. All I have to do is keep my hands off and turn my heart on.

Letting Go of Tomorrow's Decisions

I'm brand new to Al-Anon and am trying to learn

everything yesterday. I've been in the program only a short time and am newly separated from my alcoholic husband. I have little children and my parents are urging me to file for divorce. That scares me. My Al-Anon friends are suggesting I make no major decisions for at least six months, even a year. Sometimes I get so confused, and there's so much I have to attend to that I wish someone else would make decisions for me. That's when I remember to tell myself, "Let Go and Let God." I do let go, at least for a while. Each time these feelings of indecision start to overwhelm me, I use the slogan and let go for a longer time. Little by little, I can feel myself changing.

Receiving My Higher Power's Help

I grew up in an alcoholic home. Later my marriage of 25 years was progressively affected by alcoholism. I came to the mistaken belief that my husband hated and despised me. I felt so alone and friendless. I used to spend months planning ways to kill him. Finally I reached a point of insanity and decided the next time he came home he would find us all dead—our three children and me. I felt I could not go on living with a man who hated me so much, and I could not let the children live in this cruel world without me. So I mixed up four very potent poisoned milk shakes. I believe now that God intervened, because as one of the children picked up her drink, I knocked it out of her hand and poured the others down the sink. My children do not realize how lucky they are to be alive today.

Not long afterward, I threw myself off a train. Once again I believe my Higher Power was in control, for I was thrown onto the grass. I had many broken bones and was told I would never walk again. Self-pity engulfed me. I remember screaming and not being able to stop. My next recollection is of being in a padded cell in a psychiatric hospital, where I stayed for nearly three years.

A Sister in our ward took me to an Al-Anon meeting, and other members kept visiting and taking me to meetings. I used to wonder what they had to laugh about; nothing could break through the circle of self-pity I had built around me. An Al-Anon member suggested I put in some effort and get to meetings on my own. I was horrified. Wasn't I a poor little cripple?

When my husband was diagnosed with terminal cancer, like a flash of lightning into my brain came the word "Al-Anon." I thought perhaps I could help him die in peace. I didn't know that, whatever God's plan was for my husband, He had another plan especially for me that was to change my whole life. I walked back into Al-Anon and at long last, I was ready. Whatever my motives were for being there, my life had been profoundly affected by alcoholism and I needed help. At that first meeting the pain was taken from my heart and the healing tears followed.

It has not been easy. It isn't meant to be, I know. Slowly the anger, the bitterness, and self-pity (my biggest hurdle) have gone. I am learning to live my life with dignity. I can look back at all the times God stepped in to help when I was unable to ask for help, and it becomes easier to continue. Sometimes I can revert to the old pattern but I have only to bring to mind one of the Al-Anon slogans, practice it, and my life returns to peace.

Putting Myself in My Higher Power's Hands

One evening when my Al-Anon group was discussing the Fourth Step, I tried to answer my question: "Is sex a natural expression of your love?" I answered painfully and truthfully: "No! No, it isn't." Before I found Al-Anon, I used to believe all my alcoholic husband's critical remarks. And the sexually-oriented remarks were those that hurt the most. I became convinced that I was inadequate—as a friend, wife, and lover. Frigid.

God and sex have never been closely associated in my mind. Just the opposite, to be truthful. In an attempt to relax, I began to try to put myself into God's hands while lying next to my husband. My hope had been that, if I could just be a bit calmer, things would surely improve. And they did, because my attitude changed. Having put my trust in God, I no longer felt such a need to control everything that happened. As had so often happened in other areas of my life when I applied the principles I learned in Al-Anon, faith took the place of my fear. In a short time I was able to tolerate my husband's caress. As I continued to "Let Go and Let God," I was able to respond with increasing ardor, so much so that my partner asked me what had brought about the change. I don't mean to imply that I have found a magic formula for sexual enjoyment, but I do believe in changing the things I can. In my particular case, that meant putting the whole issue in the hands of God.

Trusting a Higher Power

Teenage sexual experiences with other neighborhood boys haunted me for years. I had learned very little about intimacy from my alcoholic parents. I didn't know how to express love, and I knew even less about accepting my sexual feelings and desires. I had done well in school, completed four years of military service, and was married, competent, and respected, but I still felt like an outsider until I joined Al-Anon.

Feelings of guilt and fear over my sexual desires can still keep me at a distance from other people. Always keeping my guard up, I avoid situations in which people might really get to know me, even with my wife. I see that there is a compulsive quality to my sexual feelings that I cannot control. Al-Anon has taught me that, instead of trying to control the uncontrollable, I need to trust my Higher Power: to "Let Go and Let God." I don't mean that I will close my eyes or deny that there is a problem. I mean that today, with the help of the Steps, I have a better way of dealing with my problems than ever before. I am slowly learning to accept these feelings for what they are; they do not make me a bad person, and I can get help for this problem too.

Accepting What I Cannot Change

Thank God I had been in Al-Anon for three years

when my husband was sentenced to a long prison term. My first thought on hearing of his arrest was, "How can I tell our two children?" God gave me the strength, courage, wisdom, and compassion for the alcoholic so that my attitude was not judgmental when I told the boys. By then they'd had a few years in Alateen so they were also compassionate and loving.

I prepared emotionally for my first visit to jail as though I were attending a funeral. It was painful at first, but not being able to change the situation, I began to accept it.

I live one day at a time, accepting the financial responsibility for raising our children alone. Love is sent from the prison through phone calls and letters. The children and I do talk about and with the alcoholic openly. There is no need for shame. Alcoholics go to institutions —some to hospitals and some to prison. We pull together and, thanks to Al-Anon, we have humor and love.

Letting Go of the Need to be Different

I had always wanted to be different, better than others. It comforted me to believe that I loved more, cared more, and suffered more from the effects of someone else's drinking.

I *was* different when I went to Al-Anon. I suffered from these feelings of alienation, yet while I wanted to belong, I wanted even more to remain apart—to hang on to my old life, my old thinking. I felt that as I accepted each truth, each part of the program, some portion of me was going to die. I was not capable of believing that there would be new life, that a mature woman might be born from the wreckage of a guilt-ridden, obsessive child.

My resistance remained even as I took the Steps of recovery. While I made progress emotionally through friendship and the release of some of my anxiety, I was unable to surrender myself to the idea of a Higher Power. It was many years before I made that final surrender. Then and only then did I have any idea what Al-Anon was all about. I now understand my uniqueness. There may be no one else on earth exactly like me, but with God as my partner and as a member of such a fellowship, I am not alone.

CHAPTER SIX

Practicing these Principles:
Steps Four, Five, Six, and Seven

The tools of the Al-Anon program allow us to take an active role in the sometimes slow and subtle process of acceptance. For example, Al-Anon's slogans, such as "Live and Let Live," "Easy Does It," "How Important Is It?," and "Let It Begin with Me" can often focus our attitudes in a positive direction. Constructive activities, such as involvement in Al-Anon service work, help many of us stay closely connected with Al-Anon's basic principles. They bring us into closer contact with other members of the fellowship at times when we might otherwise feel isolated.

The Fourth Step, a searching and fearless moral inventory that examines our predicament, can help sort out our feelings, choices, and responsibilities. Vague projections of disaster can be identified and challenged. We may uncover behavior or attitudes that worked to our benefit in the past but no longer serve us. We honor ourselves when we take the time to look so deeply for our truth. When we take Step Five and share what we have learned with another person as well as with our Higher Power, we demonstrate a willingness to change.

Even after we identify and admit to specific defects of character, many of us find that they still persist.

Sometimes we must accept ourselves, defects and all, before those defects are removed. As we continue to notice the effects of these attitudes and behavior patterns that no longer serve us, we take the Sixth Step, becoming entirely ready for God to remove them.

It can be humbling to discover that, though we have to do our part, we remain powerless to eliminate our defects by ourselves. Therefore we take the Seventh Step and ask for the help of our Higher Power. Many of us have found such prayer to be one of Al-Anon's most effective recovery tools. Even if we have struggled with the idea of a Higher Power, we have learned that asking for help works, no matter how much we may have doubted.

Reflections on Practicing these Principles

Focusing on Myself through Al-Anon Service

When my husband was transferred from a rehabilitation center to a state mental hospital and diagnosed as a manic-depressive, my Al-Anon Sponsor kept telling me to take the focus off him because I couldn't help him; there were professionals to do that. I should take care of me and get my own head on straight so I could help our five children. I went to five meetings a week. I felt guilty about leaving the children so much, but was anxious to feel better and find some answers.

Al-Anon did help and I worked the program with a vengeance, serving first as Group Representative, then in other capacities. I stayed deeply involved in service work because I found it so helpful to my recovery. I learned detachment and was able to tell my husband it was his choice to drink and his choice not to take his medication, but I wasn't going to sit and watch him sleep 16 hours a day when he was in depression, nor follow him around when he was manic. I wanted to live life again. I could not have survived those seven years without my Sponsor and my group's support.

Just before his last manic episode, I had made a commitment to go to an Al-Anon conference as part of my service work. I was pretty scared about how I would handle the time away at the conference. I kept saying the Serenity Prayer and saying to myself, "Just take it one day at a time." I was able to go to that conference with enough peace of mind to do my job.

To my surprise, my husband went into a mental hospital, began taking medication, and soon after immersed himself in AA as I had done with Al-Anon. I will be eternally grateful to Al-Anon for so many things, but first of all for helping me become a person again. The program showed me how to live "One Day at a Time" regardless of the circumstances. I can never give back to Al-Anon all I have gained, no matter how much I serve.

A Searching and Fearless Moral Inventory

In early attempts at the Fourth Step, I glossed over what had happened to me with a few words, such as, "I was sexually abused as a child." After overcoming a great amount of resistance within myself, I finally sat down and wrote a complete description. It was hard. In my child's mind there were no words for many of the things my father said and did, but until I put it all into words, it would continue to haunt me. My Sponsor always impressed on me that when we brings things out into the light, they lose their power over us. She was right.

As I wrote, I found that even as a very young child, I had a sense of justice and of right and wrong. I knew even then that I was being violated. As I wrote, the rage poured out in great surges, sometimes so immense that I felt capable of tearing my place apart. As soon as I completed the Fourth Step, I did the Fifth Step with another person. I then asked God to remove all the hurt and sickness from my life (the Sixth and Seventh Steps).

There has been a marked change in me since then. I no longer have bursts of blind rage. I get edgy and shout sometimes, like any person, I guess. The feeling of being out of control and a danger to others, however, has passed.

I no longer have contact with my father. I realize that although I choose to forgive him, I don't have to see him. I no longer feel constrained by the secrecy and denial that have reigned in our alcoholic family for so long. Now I feel free to get on with my own life at last.

Gaining Perspective on Strengths and Weaknesses

One mark of maturity for me in dealing with difficult situations is to decide which of my characteristics are defects and which are strengths. Al-Anon has led me to see that many times, when I take out a behavior and look at it, it's not the big monster that I feared. It may simply be "doing the best I could with what I had at the time." Knowing that I'm not always wrong gives me courage to face the criticism of others— to look at the behavior in the light of my morals. Then if I find that what they say is true, I can add it to my list for growth. If I find the criticism isn't true, I can shed it, like water off a duck's back. I don't have to accept it, but I also don't have to add to my burdens by resenting it.

Using the Slogans

Three years ago I spent 12 months in prison. My experience was horrific, one I will certainly never forget. I know now the experience was very damaging to my children, who had to cope with other children at school saying unkind things to them. My alcoholic husband couldn't handle people asking how I was coping in prison; he thought they were interfering. I felt so helpless, yet something inside me was saying, "Hang in there—'One Day at a Time.'"

I was fearful as to whether my husband and children would want me back in the house. I decided that if we had any hope of staying together as a family I had to change my lifestyle dramatically. I used "Easy Does It" and "Think" to keep my perspective. I turned to God every day and asked for His help and strength to get through the 12 months.

It is now two years since I came home. Although the going has been very rough at times, I have begun to find a new me and am very thankful to Al-Anon. It was a big relief to find people there who understood and cared. We still have the same problems with alcoholism in our home, but somehow they don't seem so big. We have a better relationship as a family now as I "Let Go and Let God," and "Listen and Learn." I don't think I could have survived without God's help or without the help I am getting from Al-Anon.

Becoming Ready to Let Go of My Defects

When I do a Fourth and Fifth Step, I list the defects

that I want God to remove, and ask, "What was the pay-off here? Why did I cling to this defect?" "In what way has it become a problem to me?" If I am not convinced that it has become a problem, I won't be willing for God to remove it. After all, I miss my defects when they are removed. I still miss the temper tantrums I used to have whenever things got tough, but I prefer the way that I handle anger today.

When I remember that change is the only way God has of making anything better, I am more willing to let it happen—even the earth-shattering change that is Al-Anon recovery.

Restoring Self-Esteem

I found out about my husband's first affair by acciden-tally finding a note the other woman had left in a wallet in our car. Feelings of disbelief and betrayal drained me of all my strength. I wasn't in Al-Anon at the time and didn't know he was an alcoholic. His drinking, women, and gambling went together. When my husband came home with lipstick on his collar, he'd confess and cry. I felt needed! At least he always came home to me.

When I think back to those days, they seem so far away. I wonder why I accepted his infidelities or his treatment of me. It seems very dramatic to say, "I accepted it because I loved him." I did love him, but didn't I love myself? Obviously I didn't love myself enough to say, "Stop it!"

In doing the Fourth Step, I came to understand that I was not responsible for what he did. I had accepted it because I had very low self-worth. Al-Anon helped me build up my self-worth. I realized that I was a wife who was loyal and willing to love in sickness and in health. If he chose another woman, he would lose more than I would. I would only be losing the heartache and a lot of foolishness, and that would be okay. Knowing my worth, I no longer accept unacceptable behavior from him.

Service Pulls Me through a Difficult Time

One more time, as it has so many times in the past 31 years, the Al-Anon program has helped me to get through a difficult situation with love, understanding, tolerance, and willingness to "Keep an Open Mind" about a condition that had been completely alien to me. My son, the star on top of my tree, told me he was gay. Nothing could have been more foreign to me or harder to confront. I sought out a support group of other parents who were dealing with the same issues and feelings, but it was Al-Anon that put me back together again. Just as Al-Anon helped me to separate the alcoholic that I loved from the choices the alcoholic made, the program helped me realize how much I loved this child, now a man, and that nothing could change that. Then I was able to be an example to the rest of the family.

Now my most heartbreaking situation is that he is HIV positive, which could develop into AIDS. I might have been pulled under, but instead my program has brought alive to me the importance of being involved. Al-Anon service keeps me always thinking program thoughts. It makes it possible for me to be cheerful while living "One

Day at a Time" with a great deal of hope, love, and gratitude for all the good things in each day.

I have more support than I ever thought possible, and
I know this is truly a gift of my Higher Power. I am sure
that without this program, I could not have appreciated
how truly wonderful my life can be in spite of difficult
situations.

Steps Four, Five, Six, and Seven

I was deathly afraid of Step Four, but my Sponsor
helped me to lay down some guidelines to follow. One
of the most important jobs was to look at all my good
points. Many of us feel foolish even trying to look for
any. I wrote down all that I like about my physical
appearance, from the top of my head to the tip of my
toes. Some of these items included my smile, the color
of my eyes, my long fingers. I next looked at what I liked
about my personality, including my ability to listen, to
care about others, to be willing, etc. I was told to list all
the people I liked, from childhood onward, and what I
liked about them. These were things that I liked about
myself or wanted to keep in my life. (I liked the school
bus driver because he always waited for me and said a
couple of extra words to me. In other words he showed
kindness and patience. Am I kind and patient? Yes,
usually, and I want to keep that in my life.) The list of
qualities soon far exceeded the list of defects, which I
explored next.

I went back into my past as far as I could and listed
on paper to the best of my memory all the people I was

angry or upset with, what had happened, and why I was mad or hurt. I likewise listed when I was afraid, the times I said something to someone else that hurt them, and times I had lied or stolen. In each situation, I questioned whether I had ever done any of the things that I resented when others did them. If so, then I was seeing myself in somebody else and didn't like it. I marked the times I was insecure, greedy, envious, or when my pride was hurt. As sex plays a big part in marriage and can be used and abused, especially in alcoholic relationships, I had to look very closely at my sexual motives. I could do something about changing myself so that these things wouldn't happen again, keeping in mind that these things are not changed overnight.

I shared my inventory with someone I trusted, and we discussed certain areas. I said, "God, this is me on this paper and I truly believe You still love me just as I am, but I know you would not be proud of some of the things on this inventory, and I certainly don't feel good about them. So with your help and me doing the footwork, maybe we can make a few changes. Thy will be done." I trusted that He would help me, in His time, in His order, and in His way. All I had to do was keep my faith strong and try to recognize these defects when they raised their ugly heads again—and, this time, try to think it through differently. I truly felt humble because I was quite helpless over these defects. I had nowhere to turn with them except to God. The emotional insecurities were the hardest. Most of my problems came from low self-esteem. My Sponsor and other Al-Anon friends had to constantly remind me that I was okay. Gradually I started reminding myself. I started to change, and my defects started to change also.

Recovering My Sanity through Service

One night, when my husband came to after an alcoholic binge, he was crazy—breaking furniture, angry, angry, angry! He demanded I give him my car keys and pushed me up against a wall when I refused. I did not want my girls to see this fight, so I sent them to their aunt's home nearby. She came immediately and tried to reason with him. Shaking and crying, I called the operator and asked her to send the police. I had to sign a paper, and then I watched them handcuff my husband and take him away. I felt numb.

At this time I had been coming to Al-Anon for probably a year. I did have the support of my group, but I did not have a Sponsor yet. I felt shy and alone. It took much love from my group for me to even survive. I did eventually find a Sponsor, or she found me. The only Step I could manage was Step One. I just used the Serenity Prayer and the slogans. I made a sign covering my refrigerator door that read, "Let Go and Let God."

God did for me what I couldn't do for myself. He got me involved in service work. I did not choose service work, I was given service work. It saved my life, my family, and my sanity.

Today I compare my husband and myself to railroad tracks—separate but going in the same direction. We allow each other to work our own programs, yet we are best friends and enjoy doing things together. Today I feel good about myself, but I still work the Steps and give service. The fellowship is where I gain strength, and the more I give the more I get. Today I feel God's love and I love life, thanks to all of you!

Becoming Entirely Ready

Even when I am willing to change, I cannot make it happen instantly. Even though Al-Anon has helped me to look not at others but at myself, I find I am as impatient with myself as I used to be with others. I want to be rid of self-centeredness; I pray about it and try to change my old thought patterns, but I'm still self-centered.

I'm frustrated! I'm trying so hard, but God hasn't fixed me yet! I wonder if one of the most important virtues God wants me to have is patience.

Maybe patience with ourselves is the middle ground between thinking we're perfectly justified in our ways and thinking we're the worst people in the world.

Al-Anon Tools are Making Me More Whole

After nine years with a violent alcoholic husband, I found myself overwhelmed with life. I had no problem accepting the word "sanity" in Step Two. Though I realize some of my actions were motivated by good intentions, much of my behavior was distorted by anger, frustration, and fear. By the time I reached Al-Anon I was a classic victim, taking my frustrations out on our four children, but very uncomfortable when I was away from home around other people. After having left "permanently" several times, I decided to give our marriage one more try with the help of Al-Anon. That was 17 years ago.

Recovery is long term and for us still a growing process. My husband's sobriety has been broken up with various drinking episodes. All three of our daughters dropped out of high school, had babies at young ages, and picked mates who are alcoholics and drug users. Our son shows signs of alcoholism. Nonetheless, Twelve Step recovery has been taking place within the family for many years now, and each of the children has been to Alateen, at least briefly. This foundation of recovery gives me hope.

These years in Al-Anon have been an adventure for me in getting to a kind of relationship with God I never dreamed possible. The Steps showed me how to connect with God by seeking His will and facing my shortcomings, trusting Him to remove them, making amends where I had done harm, and sharing with others. All my defects of character are on a shelf that only God can see totally. In each inventory I am able to see more and more of these defects. The first time I took Step Seven, I asked God to remove not only the ones I could see but any that were there. Then He began the process of taking them down one by one and doing the surgery to remove them that only He can do. The first thing He does is to make a character defect blatantly apparent to me, and then I become "entirely ready" to have it removed. Each year some of them are removed, and each year He shows me some others we have to work on.

I became active in service in Al-Anon very early. I realized that being in service made me feel obligated to maintain my own personal growth in the program, and I benefit from that obligation. The same defects that cause trouble in our homes show up in our dealings with others, so service in Al-Anon is another arena in which to discover those defects. Surrounded by the love and acceptance of my Al-Anon family, I could begin to flower—to let God untangle the qualities He had given me from their distortions.

I remember early in the program feeling like I was becoming whole and complete—the me I was meant to be—when I was around Al-Anon people and their acceptance and encouragement. I also remember crying because when I entered the door of my home I was engulfed again by gloom and discouragement. Gradually I became able to be me anywhere, including in my home. The neat thing is that "me" keeps on changing for the better.

Tools for Acceptance

I disliked sex with my husband. After I read that alcohol does affect the sex drive, I began applying the Al-Anon program. First I accepted that I was powerless over my sexual response. It would come when conditions were right and I could not will it in my own mind. Then I changed the things I could. I told my husband at a time when he could listen that I could not handle so much sex and that I would begin to refuse him, especially if he had been drinking. I told him I needed to touch him sometimes without that closeness leading to intercourse.

I asked my Higher Power to help me. I told Him that I wanted to enjoy sex with my husband and needed His help and guidance.

Next came the Fourth and Fifth Steps, which meant dealing with my own feelings and attitudes. I went to a professional counselor. The main barrier to responding to my husband was my deep anger toward him. The anger lessened when I realized that alcoholism is a disease and when I began to take care of myself and stand up for myself.

Five years after I asked my Higher Power to help me, I got answers. My husband and I faced a crisis with a sick child. For the first time in our lives we were united and supportive of each other. We turned to each other in love. I will always be grateful for this time.

Since then his alcoholism has progressed, and he has developed another disease. I am no longer sexually responding to him, but I can touch him lovingly. My program offers me the hope of being comfortable with myself; it does not promise me a happy marriage. Thanks to Al-Anon I can accept where we are and not blame my husband or myself.

Accepting Myself

During my husband's early sobriety, my only concern was that he stop drinking by whatever means. I had no thought of any need for myself, even though Al-Anon was telling me to look at myself. I was sure that if *he* straightened out, it would all work out. For a very brief period he became involved with a woman in his program. I was devastated. The good, faithful (not to mention nasty, sulky, etc.) wife had been horribly wronged! This affair, however, was the beginning of my lessened dependence on my husband, who could not be the complete source of my happiness.

But hunger is hunger; lonely is lonely. I began eating up every morsel of attention at work, just wanting to matter somewhere, to mean something to somebody. I felt entitled to love and be loved. It did not take much personal attention from men at work before I found myself having an affair. Yet I was plagued with guilt from childhood teachings of right and wrong, with a feeling of having failed in my marriage. I felt a sense of failure as one who had been given the Al-Anon program but apparently couldn't work it. I also felt the added guilt of my involvement in other innocent people's lives.

Somehow the marriage survived. Through the Steps I have understood some of the "whys" and tried to accept all elements involved. I have accepted myself as an honorable person who wants to live a good life. I have many capabilities, as well as many handicaps. "The things I cannot change" are often very real to me, and I am fully aware of my need for my program, my Al-Anon family, and for my Higher Power, who loves and forgives me when I cannot.

Taking Steps toward a Change of Attitude

I have been in Al-Anon many years and have used

the program in many difficult situations: during my husband's new sobriety, problems with the checkbook, our two sons' drinking problems, and our youngest son's attempt at suicide. But I found it hard to work my Al-Anon program when my husband's company closed down and he accepted a job earning half of what he was making before.

After two weeks I was blaming myself for what I *should* have done. We should have saved money, I should have said "no" about buying our cabin, I shouldn't have charged my holiday shopping. I called my Sponsor. I worked the Steps, for my defects and stinking thinking were robbing me of my peace of mind. I wrote down my defects in black and white: martyrdom, criticism of others, unreasonable attitudes, fearfulness, loneliness, worrying, dishonesty, and so on. As I wrote I became aware of what I could do to change them. "One Day at a Time" I can substitute positive thoughts for negative ones, praise for criticism, forgiveness for resentment, and love for hate. I've even found some gratitude: Before this new job, my husband was gone five or six nights a week and rarely at home. Now he is home every night, and we eat two meals a day together.

Al-Anon reminds me to speak with love, listen with love, and think with love. I've heard in Al-Anon that a lifetime of habits is a lifetime job to correct, but I've learned there is hope.

Assets and Defects

As an adult child of an alcoholic who later married

another alcoholic, now recovering, I had learned to focus on everyone but myself. When I went to my first Al-Anon meeting, the only way I knew how to talk to people was by criticizing others or by gossiping about them. As I have worked through the Twelve Steps of this fantastic program, I have discovered the reasons. I wanted to be noticed; I wanted to be the center of attention. I had never felt wanted. Besides, if I was talking about others, no one would ask me about myself.

Step Six and Seven were important to me. I was really ready to have God remove all of these defects of character. I had humbly asked Him to remove my shortcomings. Through my years in Al-Anon, however, one problem area remained. I had been a controller since childhood. I was finally put in a position to organize an Alateen Group, feeling all the time that I was still trying to control and not wanting to. In spite of my doubts and fears about my motives, the group fell into place easily.

One morning I mentioned to my husband how hard I had prayed for God to remove the feelings of control. He read me a prayer, asking God to remove from me every single defect that stands in the way of my usefulness to God and other people. As he read I felt as if a door were opening. I realized that God had been using my ability to organize things. All of a sudden the feelings of controlling were gone. My body felt at ease. Now when my Higher Power has a need for me to help organize, He will show me.

First Things First

I am not a person who wakes up eager to face the morning, and often the slogan, "First Things First" is what encourages me to simply get up out of bed and start my day. I experience real relief in being able to demonstrate to myself that, while I may not have a clear plan for the day, the week, month, year, or the rest of my life, I can avoid the fear and paralysis I feel when I try to take care of everything at once by just keeping it simple and living one moment at a time. I call it "doing the next thing."

"First Things First" gives me room to practice letting go on a small scale. I still have trouble applying it to pleasures—to what I want instead of what I need. I enjoy writing, for example, but I rarely make time to do it. I often think that I'll sit down to write after I have taken care of all my chores, when I have put everything in order and my life is ...perfect. Sometimes putting "First Things First" isn't getting my life in order, it's just picking up a pencil with a point.

Putting "First Things First" in troubled times often means finding whatever way I can to set aside my burdens, even if just for a moment, to make time for myself.

Taking Back My Life

I spent 22 years as a patient of a renowned psychiatrist. He was a good man, an honest man, and yet he was limited. He never mentioned that the effect that my family's alcoholism has had on my life could be a contributor to my clinical depressions, hospitalizations, or my 22 years of ingesting medications in order to make it through life! Our Al-Anon literature counsels letting go of any resentments held against clergy, doctors, and institutions. It is as necessary for my recovery as not holding resentments against my family. Although I certainly gained some insight, I now look upon this period of my life as a time when I used "ineffective coping tools," until I was blessed by the Al-Anon philosophy.

I define recovery as "taking back one's life"—knowing I am a valuable, precious human being, knowing that I have rights and can say "no," knowing that I can set boundaries no one can cross unless I invite them. I have my own personal power, which is what I retain after understanding Step One and my powerlessness over others. I am entitled to a good, happy life with support from others. I am the performing adult in my life.

These basic healthy thought patterns were acquired over a period of time by consistently and conscientiously attending Al-Anon meetings, by honest sharing with my Sponsor and others, and through service. When these activities became comfortable, I could sense I had a handle, for the first time in my life, on who I was, where I'd been, and where I wanted to go.

One of the most important words in working my program has become "process." With the help of this program and my Higher Power, I take charge of fashioning, shaping, choosing what kind of life I will have. Al-Anon has not insulated me from any additional life pains; it has not fixed the past; it gives me no guarantees. It simply gives me a message that says, "I am equal to what life presents," when I use the Twelve Steps and Twelve Traditions, the slogans, literature, sponsorship, conventions, and most importantly, meetings. Al-Anon reassures me that my life can get better—and it has, immeasurably!

Part Three

Action

CHAPTER SEVEN

Taking Care of Ourselves

The last thing on our minds in the midst of a crisis may be taking extra-good care of ourselves, but it may be our best insurance for coping with whatever may occur. It's so easy to skip a meal, gorge on junk food, or make do with too little sleep. We feel we're too busy to go to the bathroom, much less meditate. We're too busy for a meeting or to take five minutes for ourselves. We can wait forever to be in the mood for physical exercise or to find the inspiration to pray. Alcoholism is a three-fold disease—spiritual, emotional, and physical—not only for the alcoholic, but also for those of us affected by someone else's drinking. When our circumstances lead us to ignore our spiritual, emotional, or physical needs, we invite this progressive disease to take over. If we act as if our needs are unimportant, we subtly teach ourselves that we are unimportant. That's why many of us have found that it is crucial to be diligent about taking care of ourselves, especially during stressful periods. No one else can do this for us.

Taking care of ourselves may mean setting realistic goals and manageable schedules. Ten major accomplishments may be easy to achieve one day; getting out of bed might reflect our best efforts on another. We have to be flexible and realize that we are not machines. Some of us find it helpful to define clear expectations about the activities we will undertake in any given day, making sure that when we have done those things, we will stop. We can choose to let enough be enough.

With every such action we assert that we are important and that we deserve health, self-love, and self-respect, no matter what is going on in our lives. This can only make us better able to know and carry out the will of our Higher Power.

Reflections on Taking Care of Ourselves

Living a Full Life

My husband's sexual rejection of me has been the most overwhelming problem in my marriage. My husband becomes very interested in sex for a couple of nights, and then has absolutely no sexual desire for several weeks or months, even up to a year. He has repeatedly explained that his lack of desire has nothing to do with me, and that I am indeed attractive to him. His problem is a symptom of his alcoholism and depression. But that's been very hard for me to accept, and through our six years of marriage I have been very hard on myself.

Al-Anon has helped me learn to make every other area of my life as fulfilling as I possibly can. I find fulfillment in my friendships, my job, my relationship with my Higher Power, my crafts, and my music.

I am accepting the things I cannot change, as the Serenity Prayer suggests. *He* has a problem. My strong desire for a sexual relationship is normal; I'm okay; it's all right to feel frustrated about it. When frustration starts to dominate my thoughts, I try to change the things I can. I deliberately turn to some activity that will help me change my attitude and feel glad to be alive—attending Al-Anon meetings, shopping, reading a good book, or roller skating with a friend. I also devote much time and energy to helping others through Al-Anon service work. I do not turn to these activities in order to stuff my feelings or pretend that no problem exists. Accepting reality includes accepting that if I don't do something, I become depressed and unbearable to live with—for my husband and, more importantly, for me. Therefore, I get plenty of sleep. I can handle my emotions better when I'm rested. I take care of myself physically, dress well, exercise, and eat right.

I've stopped trying to figure out why he is the way he is. Further analysis of the problem is a waste of valuable time and becomes a good excuse to feel sorry for myself.

Our sexual relationship is only one area of my life. I'm not saying that this is an easy situation to accept, but my changed attitude and actions can make it much easier.

Finding Time for Myself

When I was a new Al-Anon member, I reviewed my schedule, wondering how and where I could find time to practice keeping the focus off of the alcoholic and on myself. (At that time I had five children—the youngest a newborn—and I worked full-time in a job that required me to bring work home.) A longtime Al-Anon member remarked that any little bit of time I could devote to reading our literature, attending meetings, telephoning other members, and reflecting upon what I had learned would be a positive step in the right direction. I tried her suggestion and it worked. Focusing on program material for as little as three minutes at a time helped me settle my leaping mind and still my apparent need to keep moving. As I slowed down, so did my children. Even the baby became less fussy.

Recognizing My Need to Relax

I came into Al-Anon because my lover went into AA, and I wanted to help and support her sobriety. When I heard that the best way to help her was to work on myself, I left. A year later I realized that I was spending almost every waking moment focusing on her while my own life was falling apart. I crawled back to Al-Anon.

I got a Sponsor and started working the Steps. I learned to share in meetings, to use the phone, and to begin to detach from my lover's disease. Gradually I began to feel better.

One day my Sponsor asked me what I did to relax and have fun, and I had no answer. I didn't "waste" my time on frivolity, I was working on myself! The energy that had been focused on my lover—to make her change—was now focused on rooting out character defects and dissecting everything about my past—to make me change. My Sponsor pointed out that while it was appropriate to give my Al-Anon recovery top priority, the Steps make it clear that the actual healing changes would come from God, not from me. I saw that I was depriving myself of simple, healthy pleasures because I thought I would heal faster that way. In reality, I was powerless to control the pace of my recovery.

I began to find ways of taking care of myself. I feel grateful that I learned these things before my lover decided to move out. In the devastating months that followed, I needed the self-care and comfort that I had begun to believe I deserved. For example, at low moments (there were times when I felt suicidal) I found that creativity was a great antidote for negativity. I had been a sculptress, but one of the effects of alcoholism was that I lost touch with my art for several years. The idea of working in my studio overwhelmed me. So I did what I could. I invented recipes for chicken and garnished the plate with flowers. I bought a coloring book and a set of markers. I made up song lyrics.

Going to coffee after meetings was extremely helpful. The breakup had left me feeling rejected and unlovable. The warm support I received in these social evenings helped with those feelings and filled many otherwise lonely hours. Hot showers, dancing in front of my mirror to very loud music, a cuddly teddy bear, and especially exercise lifted my spirits. Once a month I went to a comedy club with an Al-Anon friend, just to remind myself that no matter how tragic my life seemed, some things were still funny. I bought a blank book, and when my feelings were bottled up inside, I would write a letter to this God I was trying to understand, as if I were writing to a new friend.

To my surprise, none of these activities interfered with my Al-Anon recovery. Ironically, the answer to a problem I had struggled with for months appeared to me in the middle of a movie. In other words, the answer came when I "Let Go and Let God." Today I know that part of my recovery is respecting my need and my right to let go and relax.

Attending to My Spiritual Needs

This year God seems to be working on my management of time. God gave us all 24 hours in each day. It's not reasonable to think I have to have more or can't take time to sleep.

In the early days of my recovery, I had little energy left over after trying to do battle with alcoholism on my own. Al-Anon meetings helped me to take the First Step and admit I was powerless over alcohol, acknowledging that this was a battle I would always lose. After a while I began to have energy for other things, but I got to the point where I was throwing my life and will at God as I charged off into each day. I was doing without much-needed quality time with Him. He found ways to let me fall on my face, and now I'm back on track again.

Al-Anon literature helps me to remember to take care of my spiritual needs. This is how I stay in touch with the Second Step, knowing that sanity comes from my Higher Power. In my case this means dedicating the first Monday of each month to actively improving my conscious contact with God. I hibernate in my room and don't take any calls, and God and I spend time together. I work on the Steps, read, pray, and just be with my God.

D.L. Moody once said, "We ought to see the face of God every morning before we see the face of man. If we have so much business to attend to that we have no time to pray, depend on it, we have more business than God ever intended we should have." Life is so full. There is so much that needs to be done, but I want to be doing what God wants me to do.

Doing for Myself

My spouse is spending these 25 hours in jail for driving under the influence of alcohol. This is a first for him. Though his drinking has been a problem for more than 25 years, he's never been arrested before.

After two years of sobriety he returned to drinking "just a little." The difference this time is that I don't have to regress with him, unless I choose to do that. Sometimes I fall into self-pity—I forget he has an insidious disease—but I know where to go for help. So does he.

I spend a great deal of time these days talking with my Sponsor, and I go to more Al-Anon meetings than ever. I'm also doing what I can to make myself more comfortable—taking hot baths, giving myself flowers, and keeping busy with the things that interest me. I'm sorry my spouse is in jail tonight. I can't imagine how it must be, but if that's what he has to go through to regain sobriety, then he must. I hope he'll get sober in time. Meanwhile, I'm grabbing hold of every moment of serenity and keeping my head above water—sometimes just barely, but that's okay, that's all it takes.

It's a far cry from when I arrived in Al-Anon. Now, the bright days far outnumber the dark ones.

Getting My Priorities in Order

Learning to budget money and time seem to go hand in hand for me—learning to be neither a penny pincher nor a spendthrift. When my focus was on the alcoholics in my life, this kind of middle ground seemed impossible to achieve. Because of Al-Anon I see that if I am to find a balance, I need to learn to get my priorities in order. I have to learn to plan reasonably, allowing for necessities first (including a reserve for emergencies), then luxuries. I must also be aware of which is which: my Al-Anon program is not a luxury—it is a necessity.

Learning to Give Myself Love

Sometimes I hear the quiet sobbing of this lonely child who is still a part of me. What she longs for now is no different than what she wanted then—a hug, a touch, a smile. How I dreaded the morning after a drinking bout: blood dried on the carpet, my mother's broken nose, blackened eyes hiding behind sunglasses in the dead of winter. Pieces of dishes were scattered, as if pieces of my heart lay broken on the cold floor. And so I lie weeping, reliving a nightmare I will not wake from, for I am not asleep.

The reassurance which never came is still most often withheld; no longer from all-important Mom and Dad, but from all-important *me*. How often I scorn this lonely child I was, and sometimes still am. I belittle her "weakness," turn my back on her pain. It's so easy to intellectualize her hurting and unmercifully judge the validity of her feelings. She doesn't need a lecture, she needs love. She doesn't need a kick, she needs a caress. She doesn't need accusations, she needs acceptance. At the very time she needs me most, I've treated her coldly, with contemptuous indifference, causing the burning in her eyes and the aching in her heart to deepen.

There are times now, if I am still enough to listen, that I hear her weeping. Her pain causes me great sadness, for she's suffered so much. Then, because of all I have learned in Al-Anon, I reach out my hand to her, help her to her feet, wipe the tears from her eyes, and gently hold her.

Doing Whatever I Can

I have only been in Al-Anon 18 months, and for the last eight months I have not been black-and-blue nor had a broken bone. My husband is still drinking, worse really, but the bad times are not there anymore because I don't participate.

I went to my first Al-Anon meeting with a black eye and my left arm broken. No one at the meeting asked what happened or commented on how I looked. They only showed that they were glad I was there! One of the first things I heard was to be good to myself, so I made an appointment with a doctor and had my arm set and put in a cast. Later I was able to look for a job.

My husband is still a very angry person, but today I let him be responsible for his own actions. I do not take on his guilt. A few times I have had to get out of the house fast. Twice I have had to call the police, but I have followed through with going to court, hanging onto my Sponsor's hand and praying every step of the way. My Higher Power has given me whatever I needed for that day.

My husband knows I intend to do whatever I can to protect myself. I always knew someday God would have a better place for me. I did not dream it would be in this life, at an Al-Anon meeting just four blocks from my house.

Being Good to Myself

Not too long into the Al-Anon program I had my first experience with my Higher Power. The previous evening I had been awakened and hauled out of bed, to drunken accusations that I was ignoring my husband by pretending to be asleep. Now he was late coming home, and I wondered if there would be a repeat of the night before. I knew I had to work my program. What could I be doing so I wouldn't be worrying? "Be good to yourself," they had said. I practiced my guitar, watched a movie, and did the mending in peace. My Higher Power intervened and told me "It's time to go upstairs now." I got ready for bed, although it was still early. I thought of how I had not been allowed to read in bed for five years, and here was my chance—how wonderful! Again, after a while, the inner voice said, "Turn off the light." I obeyed and lay there with a sense of gratitude for a wonderful evening.

Listening to My Body and My Mind

My journey of self-discovery in Al-Anon has been intensified by the Fourth Step inventories and Fifth Steps I have taken, but it isn't limited to that. It is a continuing, ongoing process. It includes physical aware-ness; I have had to learn to listen to my body. I tend to stay in my head so much that this is still difficult for me.

I have to make a real effort to change, but I am learning. After all, my body not only tells me what it needs, but it tells me how I feel. I don't know what I need unless I know how I feel. I have to pay attention to physical messages and manifestations. I sometimes ignore the most obvious ones. For instance, I keep going when I'm tired—and going and going. I sometimes eat when I am not hungry. I often miss the subtler messages entirely.

I also have to pay attention to how I feel because I believe that God guides me through feelings. But I need to stay aware of what I am thinking as well. My thoughts can create my reality. And words! Words are tremendously powerful. An awareness of what I say not only helps me to eliminate negativity from my conversations (and thereby my thoughts and thereby my life), but also makes me conscious of the possible ways in which others might hear me.

Making It My Business to Enjoy Life

Until I came into Al-Anon I was unaware of the connection between personality changes, lying, infidelity, squandering money, resentment of our baby, and drinking. Since my mother had died when I was five, I wanted very much to have an "intact" family and was willing to give everything I had to make it work. I almost gave my life. In the past I had been able to remove myself from abusive situations, but this time I was stuck. My husband insisted that he loved his new girlfriend and had never loved me. I couldn't just "lose his phone number" because we had a child and I was very close to his family.

Everyone was supportive of me, but I started to die of a broken heart nonetheless. I only wanted my husband, my dream, my family. I lost weight and started smoking cigarettes. I obsessed around the clock on how to fix the marriage, on what was wrong and what strategy I could use, and on feelings of rejection. I cried for hours and hours every day, slept from two to four hours a night, and had chronic digestive problems. I ate erratically, threw up after talking to a divorce lawyer, and barely functioned on any level, though I worked in my profession and somehow raised my child through all this.

I found Al-Anon almost by accident and embraced it with the zeal of a drowning woman. I realized that I could not change the past, get rid of the girlfriend (they are still living together), move away, or get my husband into recovery. I was the one who was suffering, I was the one who was dying inside, and therefore I was the one who had to change. I had little self-esteem and didn't really think it made any difference what I said, did, or wanted. Al-Anon gave me the awareness that what I felt did matter. I went to many meetings, read the *One Day at a Time in Al-Anon* book every day, started to share and cry at meetings, and reached out to people. I listened, studied the Steps and slogans, and read everything. I also made a commitment to private therapy. I have learned to focus on myself and to develop self-esteem by feeling my feelings and doing things I believe in. I now pray everyday, eat three meals, exercise, and devote myself to the work I love and to my recovery. I receive nurturing through my senses and make it my business to enjoy my life.

Nothing has altered in the situation that precipitated this change of attitude. I have no relationship with my husband. I have had to let go and accept everything in that area. I failed entirely to fix the situation. The difference is that I have changed. I have hope for myself and my son. I do not live in fear. I trust that as the bitterness fades, I will have a chance to love again and to let someone love me for my real self.

CHAPTER EIGHT
Decision-Making and Change

Change is risky, but there often comes a time when we know that action must be taken and decisions made. Whether we are considering a confrontation or a lawsuit, seeking therapy, opening a checking account, getting or quitting a job, writing a letter of amends, filing for divorce, choosing to wait a while before making a particular decision, getting married, or anything else, making decisions can be a challenge.

Past decisions may have been made hastily, carelessly, or fearfully. In Al-Anon, many of us find it important to examine our motives as well as our options when facing decisions. Are we able to see our actions clearly, or are our minds clouded by the effects of someone else's drinking? Is this choice a reaction to provocation? Having been pushed, are we pushing back almost by reflex? Is this an effort to control or to exact punishment to pay someone back for our suffering? Are we trying to do for others what they should do for themselves? Are we bowing to other people's values or opinions, trying to please them without regard for our own opinions or desires? In other words, is the disease of alcoholism motivating this action, leading us away from self-esteem and a healthy attitude? Or is this action motivated by a sense of rightness within, a reasonable conviction that this is the best choice to be made at the present time under the present circumstances—and therefore a choice stemming from a healthy state of mind? Al-Anon never suggests that we have to be "all better" before we can make decisions. In fact, most of us must accept that our motives are rarely completely pure. In Al-Anon, however we are encouraged to be as honest as possible about the decision-making process and to talk it over with other members of the fellowship.

Not all of us have the luxury of choosing the timing. A court date will not be postponed just because we haven't been inspired to show up. Foreclosure won't be delayed because we remain emotionally attached to our home. If we are in a potentially dangerous situation, it may be essential to take immediate action, regardless of how we feel about ourselves or the other people involved. We may never have the choices we would have if we were writing the script, but we always have choices. We can, as the Serenity Prayer says, accept the things we cannot change and change the things we can, one day at a time. Especially, we can begin to change our attitudes.

There is no formula for when and how to act. We must each decide for ourselves. No one else can define our role in the unique partnership we develop with our Higher Power. If we have given our will and our lives to that Higher Power, whatever choices we make can be used for our growth. If we are unsure, we can ask again for guidance. Then it is up to us to get quiet enough to listen to the answers we receive, trusting that our feelings, thoughts, and actions will be guided by a Power greater than ourselves.

Reflections on Decision-Making and Change

Taking Time to Make Decisions

Forgiveness . . . Detachment . . . Acceptance . . . Three key words in the Al-Anon program. Yet different interpretations of these words can lead to different choices. Most of the people I have met in the program have chosen to continue living with the alcoholic in their life. My own marriage hit a crisis point about five years ago. I became depressed, confused, and unable to concentrate. I seemed to be crying all the time, not really understanding what was wrong. My life seemed directly tied to the alcoholic. I felt like a yo-yo, with him pulling my string. Our relationship deteriorated, and the distance between us increased. The real crisis hit when his infidelity became an issue in our lives; the pain was overwhelming.

It was not feasible for me to make a decision about my marriage during this crisis time. I was often ambivalent. I would caution anyone like myself involved in making a major decision to feel comfortable with taking time to do so. It wasn't until I had been in Al-Anon for quite a while that I felt able to consider the possibility of a divorce.

When I did, several issues haunted me:

The idea of breaking up the family unit was something

I couldn't accept. I was concerned that my decision would scar my children's lives forever. Would they ever forgive me? Would my spouse fight for custody?

How could I continue to pay bills? Would I have to move? Would we really be "poor," as my children feared?

Being alone was scary for me. Everyone enjoys a day or evening alone to do whatever they choose, but an endless string of such days and evenings is something else. I became aware of the emotional dependence I had on the alcoholic. I had always prided myself on being independent and yet found myself frightened of the prospect of being alone. Who would be there for me? Who would share in celebrating my successes or be there on a bad day to comfort me and hug me? Would I ever date again? Would I always be alone?

Divorce was an unacceptable alternative in my religion. Would I have to give up my faith? Could the God of my childhood understand? My marriage vows kept ringing in my ears.

In the midst of all this confusion, I was fortunate to have Al-Anon. I learned to focus on myself, to become self-caring. My self-esteem grew with the love I received from fellow members. I "listened and learned." I can remember searching the *One Day at a Time in Al-Anon* book for something to guide me in my decision, and I found it on page 86: "Acceptance does not mean submission to a degrading situation. It means accepting the fact of a situation, and then deciding what we will do about it."

In Al-Anon I was able to work through my anger. I forgave...I detached...and finally accepted. Then two years ago I made the decision to divorce the alcoholic in my life. I have never once regretted that choice. I have my own life now—a peaceful one. The children seem okay. I was promoted just before the alcoholic left our home, so money is not as much an issue as I thought it might be. I am not alone. My friends in and out of the Al-Anon program are always there when I need them. My friendships have grown far beyond my expectations, and I feel very fortunate. I waited and waited for the spiritual awakening that so many Al-Anon friends described, but have found that my own sense of spirituality has been awakened more slowly. Nonetheless, I am grateful that my relationship with my Higher Power is more personal today than it ever was before this crisis.

Making Firm Decisions about Enabling

I remember sitting in Al-Anon meetings and hearing others say that, in effect, working the program required a different dimension of effort if the alcoholic were your child. I thought that was so much hogwash. At the time I was engrossed in getting my sanity back after living with an alcoholic husband who was then in the early stages of recovery. My children were grown, and their old, unresolved anger towards me kept them distant. In retrospect I realize that not having to deal with their issues while trying to repair a damaged marriage was a break for me, although at the time I was so eager for us to be a viable family unit that I sometimes came across as slightly fanatical.

It was inevitable that I would hear about the problems my son was having with his temper, his fists, and driving under the influence. Eventually he sought treatment. Afterwards, because I believed his desire for sobriety was sincere, I cosigned a note so he could buy a car and get to AA meetings. He made only a few payments and never attended a meeting.

Wintry weather arrived early that year, and soon he was behind in his rent and facing eviction. If I had learned nothing else from Al-Anon, I knew I had to let him experience the consequences of his own actions or inactions. I declined to help him, and within a short time he was sleeping in his car. The nights were bitter cold—well below freezing.

That's when the full impact of the subtle differences between having an alcoholic spouse and an alcoholic child hit me. My son was a young man of 25, but I thought of him as a montage of all the ages he's been. How could I let the innocent little boy within him sleep on the streets? I hung tough. My Sponsor supported me. I shared about it in meetings. I prayed for wisdom, guidance, and strength.

My recovering husband surprised me one day when he suggested I offer the young man a cash loan, enough for a deposit and first month's rent, and then make it clear there would be no more. "Either he makes it or he doesn't, but this way you'll know you did all you could."

With silent apologies to the nameless Al-Anon parents I had once felt superior to, I jumped at the chance, the permission, to stake my son to yet another fresh start. Before long he was in trouble again. He totaled his car and served time in jail. My conscience was clear, though, and since then I've had no problem detaching with love—and without money.

Following Through

I never expected to have abuse in my marriage. When it occurred, I was shocked, ashamed, and fearful. I altered my behavior so I wouldn't upset the alcoholic. Thus, the fear of his abuse controlled me. After two years in Al-Anon it became intolerable. I signed a complaint, and my husband was arrested.

I prayed constantly. I put my life in God's hands. I called an AA friend and asked her to get somebody to talk to my husband. I went to police headquarters and told my husband I could no longer live with the abuse or his drinking. He said he would stop. I didn't buy that, but I told him if he went to AA and stopped drinking I'd stay.

He did, but that's not the end of the story. I still had a court date ahead of me. My husband pressured me to drop the charges. I was tempted. He was now in AA, I was in Al-Anon, and I wanted it all behind me. Something told me to follow through on what I had started. I went before the judge, and I asked God to give me the words to say. I said I wanted some reassurance that my husband would continue to get help. The judge told him he must continue going to AA.

I know that I had him arrested not to punish him, but for my own protection. It was the hardest thing I had ever done in my whole life, but my self-esteem had grown enough through the program that I would no longer accept abuse. I knew I was worthwhile. Had I not been actively practicing my program, I would never have had the courage to take those steps and stand by my action.

Choosing to Be Myself

Many of us have relationships that are essentially based on fear of loss. We choose what we do and what we say with an eye and an ear to keeping the other person around. I was brought up with a Deep South tradition that said, "Let him win. Make him feel important." What I heard was, "Be less than you can be, or you won't be loved." I know now that anyone who loves me wants me to be all that I can possibly be, but that was a lesson a long time in coming. I am not talking about being competitive; I am talking about spiritual seeking and spiritual growth, developing into whatever it was that God had in mind when He created me. Healthy people do not sacrifice themselves for the sake of someone else's ego.

I am not an alcoholic, but I do have the family disease myself, because I have been affected by other people's alcoholism. As long as I use this disease as an excuse, it is nearly as convenient as using someone else's disease. This is like saying, "I've discovered that I have diabetes, and as soon as I feel better, I am going to start taking insulin." When I hear myself saying, "Of course I'm afraid that I'll be abandoned—that's true of many of us who have been affected by alcoholism," Al-Anon helps me remember that today I have a choice. I can decide not to wait until the fear is gone to start my recovery. Instead I can try to apply the Twelve Steps to my life. That way there is hope that, as I recover in Al-Anon, my fear will diminish.

Finding Healthier Reasons to Act

Both my parents were alcoholics. My father died when I was 15. He had told me to take care of my mother. After his death, no matter what I said to my mother, she always asked, "Where's the money?" When I got married the first thing my wife asked was, "Where's the money?" I got the picture that if I could provide money for my mother she wouldn't drink; if I would provide money for my wife she would be happy. I was always out there trying to earn more.

I had made an assumption that if I have money I'm a man, and if I don't, I'm not. The greatest benefit of coming into Al-Anon was in learning to accept myself as I am.

Prior to Al-Anon, I confronted problems and never discussed their root causes. I thought that knowing the underlying causes wouldn't help me. Now I realize that many of these false assumptions resulted from living with alcoholism. Al-Anon helps me take a fresh look at myself, my problems, and my beliefs. I pray for knowledge of God's will and the power to carry that out. *Then*

I go out and earn, and feel good about it.

Recognizing and Making Choices

To me, Al-Anon means that I have choices. I have spent years thinking that my life was controlled by the choices of the people around me. When my husband would do something that hurt my feelings, I never dreamed I could choose not to be offended by it. When my alcoholic child decided not to use the tools he had been given for sobriety, I couldn't believe I could choose to maintain my own serenity.

Recently my ex-daughter-in-law disappeared with my three-year old grandson. The old me would have taken it very personally. I did initially, but thanks to my Al-Anon group, I realized that she did what she thought was best for her and the child. I miss being able to see him, but I know he is loved and well cared for. God willing, I will be reunited with him some day soon.

The old me would have become sick with resentment and the pain of loss. The healthier me has been able to turn loose and live just "One Day at a Time." I now choose to trust that my Higher Power will not give me more than I can handle.

When the Time Was Right, the Choice Became Clear

After 18 months of prayerful reflection in this program, I decided I no longer wanted to live with active alcoholism. I moved out on my wife of 27 years amidst anger and hurt feelings.

Although my life became simpler, it was not more

tranquil. I had set a six-month time limit for deciding between reconciliation and divorce. Daily, it seemed, I alternated between critical re-examination of my motives and self-bashing for being a quitter. I felt like I had flunked Al-Anon. Through Al-Anon literature, prayer, and meditation, I was assured that answers would come when needed. In spite of what I knew, I compulsively replayed the "what ifs" in mind: "If she doesn't get sober, what is the outcome?" "If she gets sober, what..."

One morning after four months of separation, the answer came in an unexpected way. Seemingly out of nowhere, two hypothetical questions popped into my mind which permitted me to reframe my situation and perceive my root values. The first: What would I do with my life if I won the lottery? The second: What would I do if I had only six months to live and would remain in good health? When I used these questions to try to identify what I really wanted in my life, I saw that continuing in my marriage had no place there.

My wife's sobriety or lack of it never was the issue. Our diverging paths these many years have led us toward different value systems. The question has become, "How do I want to pursue my spiritual development?" My answer is that I can't return to that life and continue my spiritual growth. The old life and the old relationship were toxic to both our spirits.

Through the Al-Anon program I have learned that my paramount responsibility is my spiritual growth. With the constant guidance of the program and by the grace of my Higher Power, that journey continues.

Taking Action and Sitting Still

As an adult child of an alcoholic, I felt I must be worthy to be loved and tried to earn love. I was always doing something.

If someone hurt, I would do something for them, but could not be there for them. If I wasn't doing something, I felt uncomfortable. I became so involved in finding things to do that I couldn't sleep well. My mind was planning things to do or worrying about things I did.

At an Al-Anon meeting I heard, "God made us human beings, not human 'doings.'" That has helped me evaluate my activities. I don't have to be doing something all the time. I can just be. I have found by *being* I can enjoy the present, living "One Day at a Time."

Believing I'm All Right

Just a month after the death of our six-month old baby girl, I found I was pregnant again. I was so happy, but the "what ifs" were holding back much of my joy: What if something happens to this baby?

My husband got worse with his drinking and using, and moved out. He assured me it was just until he could get a better hold on his life, and that he would be there for me when the baby came. I was terrified I couldn't do this alone so I called my Al-Anon friends, who kept my spirits up.

The baby was long overdue, and eventually the doctor wanted to induce labor. I asked my husband to be there on Thursday, but he said, "No, I can't leave—they need me here." I made it through the rest of the conversation with tears streaming down my face. He said, "I'll call you tomorrow night" and hung up. I cried till I thought I'd turn myself inside out. I asked God, "How can this be? I can't do this! I'm afraid!" For hours I lay there asking God, "Why?" Suddenly it was as if my Higher Power said, "Now if you'll only listen to me, you're all right. You can do this." I had heard so many Al-Anon members share in meetings about learning that they were all right. They said that it happened as they worked the Steps and got to know and trust a Higher Power. At this difficult time I began to believe it myself.

The next day labor started all on its own. I drove myself to the hospital, checked myself in, and brought a 9lb., 6 oz. baby girl into this world. When they finally left me alone with my new daughter, all my fears, hurts, anger, and emptiness came over me, but not as long this time. My husband didn't know he had a new baby girl till she was two days old because he didn't call that night for reasons of his own. The day the baby and I went home from the hospital, I made the decision to load up the car and move out. I never would have made it without Al-Anon and my Higher Power. I had learned I was all right!

Taking a Stand

The agony of indecisiveness tortured me before I entered Al-Anon. I thought that the decision I needed to make was whether or not to stay in a relationship with the alcoholic. But one morning I realized that, with all that had happened to me because of alcoholism, I needed help, so I called Al-Anon.

I had been battered several times, each time thinking it would be the last. The alcoholic finally told me he could not guarantee that it would not happen again. I understood and used what Al-Anon had taught me: the knowledge that I have choices. I came to believe I was keeping a very sick secret with the alcoholic, so I revealed the violence at a meeting and also contacted an outside agency. All my life I had solved my problems by running away: I had run away from every major relationship in my life. The alcoholic told me that if I left he would find me, and I believed him. With God's great compassion for me, He had put me in a situation from which I could not run away.

Al-Anon helped me to focus my attention on what I could do about my situation, instead of concentrating all my attention on what I thought the alcoholic should do. I was the one who had to take a stand. I would not be driven from my home by my fear, but would do whatever was necessary to change the things I could change. After the next incident of violence, I pressed charges. I thank my Higher Power that He had a plan, and because I did my part, He could do His. While not everyone emerges from a violent situation with a happy, non-violent relationship, in my case the alcoholic also faced himself. He received counseling and the incidents have never been repeated.

Healing While Hurting

A friend once said, "Some folks seem to be able to skip

through life, bouncing comfortably on the surface, with little trouble—and then there are those of us who must dig into life and come up with it all over our hands and faces." The longer I am in Al-Anon, the more deeply I dig into life. It continues to cause pain, but the joys far outweigh everything else! I have learned that my Higher Power can use my unwise decisions to teach me and that He will sustain me through the aftermath. Some decisions are not simply choices between something good and something not-good, but are more like: "Which kind of pain can I live with most readily?" I have found that this applies to every area of my life, including my marriage to a recovering alcoholic. There are times when I have to hurt through a situation. When this happens, the choice is not whether to hurt or not to hurt, but what to do while I am hurting. I can function productively while I heal or I can turn my face to the wall and hide a while. I have done some of both, but at least I know now that I have the choice.

Taking Time to Decide

I've been asked by my spouse to take on a big responsibility, one I don't know if I can handle. I agree it needs to be done, but when I'm really honest with myself, I don't want to do it. I want to do God's will, but I'm not sure what He wants me to do. It scares me that He might want me to tackle this job.

My Sponsor tells me to take a while to decide (more than the two to three days my spouse suggested). She said to make a decision about what's right for me, not one designed to please my recovering alcoholic husband or to relieve any fear of disapproval from others. She suggested making a list of pros and cons. I've often heard that if we make a decision we feel is right for us, it will be right for everyone concerned.

Another Al-Anon friend told me that when she is faced with a comparable situation, she tells God she doesn't want to do it, and if He wants it of her, would He please put the desire in her heart? So that is what I tell God every morning.

Changing the Way I React

I was born with my left arm missing below my elbow. Even though I knew I could not change that, I was mentally destroying myself over other people's reactions, no matter what they might be! The disease of alcoholism had taught me to be quite a people-pleaser. Al-Anon helped me to accept the fact that, although I have no control over other people's reactions or thoughts, I *can* change the way I react. It works! Everyday I say, "God can change my reactions, and I'm finally willing to let Him, with no interference from me."

I did not realize how much Al-Anon worked for me until I was leaving a meeting recently. My husband said, "Honey, did you get upset again when your group joined hands to pray?" That's when I realized that during the prayer I had actually been praying, instead of worrying about the lady on my left and how she must be reacting to holding my deformed arm. If Al-Anon thinking can change something that "big" in my life, then I know it can change every resentment, every guilt, and all other mental and spiritual ailments I have.

Doing What's Right for Me

The loneliness of being married and living together in the same house and sleeping in the same bed, yet being separated by an invisible wall, was worse than living alone in my own apartment and sleeping in a single bed. I have been on my own for ten months now, and the freedom I feel in my inner person is indescribable. It's so good not to be struggling to survive the fear of the emotional and physical abuse that resulted from my husband's alcoholism.

My 24-year old daughter recently called me long-distance and asked what I'd been doing. I immediately launched into a defensive explanation, listing the things I did after school and why I had gotten home late that evening. She said, "Mom, you are a big girl, and you can do what you want; you don't owe me an explanation." This incident really made me aware of how trapped I had felt in my marriage. As I have heard in so many Al-Anon meetings, I don't have to justify my actions.

I had never considered divorce an option. I figured I was tough and could endure anything, especially with the gift of strength from my Higher Power. In Al-Anon I saw others working the program and surviving in healthy ways in their sick marriages. I also saw couples who were in counseling and happy to be establishing a healthy relationship. Thus, I felt guilty when I realized I was going to have to choose a different path and leave my husband. I believe that both partners need to be willing to do the hard work it takes for each to become healthy individuals, and then to work together and support each other in building a healthy relationship.

A few months ago I was willing to settle for less than my fair share of our assets in the divorce settlement because I wanted to put an end to this mess. But I didn't feel good accepting compromises that weren't fair. Therefore I have hired a more assertive lawyer, who is helping me stand up for my rights. While Al-Anon is helping me to survive daily, it is also encouraging me to lay the groundwork for a healthy future by working at maintaining a healthy attitude and self-esteem during this time of not knowing the final results. It doesn't matter so much how the details of the settlement turn out, but my serenity and growth in the process are what determine successful results.

Free to Make Choices

Al-Anon has been synonymous with freedom for me. It has broken chains that had me shackled—chains put in place by living with someone who has the disease of alcoholism. They were chains with links made of other people's rules, other people's opinions, old guilt, and old resentments. One by one, these chains have been broken or are being broken in Al-Anon, and I am more free all the time. When I become aware of the freedom in a given area and am able to make choices that I never knew were possible, I usually realize that I could have been free all the time if I had only recognized it.

This fact was graphically brought to my mind when my husband and I went out to feed a friend's dog while our friend was out of town. The dog is a big German shepherd who is kept in a backyard with a four-foot fence around it. When he was a puppy, he tried to jump the fence and found that he couldn't. He has never learned that he can now jump it any time he wants. He thinks he is still hemmed in by something bigger than he can handle. He is confined by his own perceptions.

Doing What I Feel Is Right

My son is an alcoholic. For several years he and a sweet girl lived together, and eventually they had a baby. As his drinking got worse, so did their fighting. Finally the girl had enough, so she took the baby and moved out. My son found where she was staying and roughed her up, giving her bruises and a black eye. She decided to press charges, but the weather was bad and she had no car. She accepted my offer to drive her to the courthouse. I also took photos of her bruises and gave them to her. In spite of court delays, the charges stuck.

Some people wondered how I could help her press charges against my son. I thought about "being loyal to one's own" and other "shoulds" and "guilt trips," but I realized that, given the same circumstances, I'd have supported any other Al-Anon friend. In Al-Anon I have learned that no one but I can determine what I should or should not do. I thank the program for giving me the strength to do what I believe is correct.

Rejecting Unacceptable Behavior

Alcoholism is a disease that takes many forms. My spouse chooses to make food his battleground. All of his outrage, resentment, and bad feelings are poured out upon any meal which is placed before him. As his disease progresses, the strictures become limiting.

We were never to have vegetables in the house again—or fruit. He never wanted to see chicken again—or ham—or casseroles. Ice cream was never to be served at noon and waffles never at night. No day was free of contention.

I was frantic. Some evenings I cooked three or four dinners hoping to win his approval. He rarely gave it. Breakfasts were a nightmare. I came to believe that if I could only learn to fry eggs without breaking the yolk, he would never drink again. He told me so!

Al-Anon has taught me that I can take care of myself and that I am not obligated to accept unacceptable behavior. I cannot control his behavior, but I don't have to allow it to incapacitate me. I have made some choices that help me to live more sanely. I have stopped getting up for breakfast. I am no longer willing to start my day with such negative overtones. One dinner at a time is enough. Today I cook for me. I do offer him a choice: eat or don't eat.

There is sobriety in our home today, for which I am truly grateful. The food situation has not changed. A friend who is a dietician told me that excessive drinking can destroy taste buds. When my spouse complains that everything he eats tastes like sawdust, he may be right.

That is not my problem. I know today that I am not a bad or incompetent person because he doesn't like his meals. I remind myself that if he said I was a chair, it would not make me a chair. I am a worthwhile person. My friends in Al-Anon tell me they love me anyway, whether I break egg yolks or not.

Flexible Decision-Making

Some of us came to Al-Anon so lacking in self-confidence that we thought we couldn't do anything. We were incapable of making the simplest decisions for ourselves, yet could tell others how to run *their* lives.

I have to grow enough to listen to others' suggestions and realize that they are just suggestions. The choices and decisions are up to me. Even if I consult a professional, I still have to decide whether or not to accept the opinion. This would be informed decision-making: asking for and receiving suggestions, listing my alternatives and the probable realistic outcome, then making decisions based on the best information that I can gather.

Decision-making must also have flexibility. When I came to Al-Anon I was such a rule follower. I was so ramrod unbending, it was difficult for me to learn to roll with the punches.

I went through a stage of being a people-pleaser, then reached another when I thought, "Well, I'll do whatever I want to and if they don't like it that's their problem." Now, however, I have learned that my decisions do sometimes affect others, and I try to take them into consideration.

Choosing a Different Response

There were many times after my husband stopped drinking and went into AA that I thought I would wear out detachment, the Serenity Prayer, Al-Anon literature, and the phone. Moments of serenity were just that—moments. Then in the middle of behaving as if he were in a "dry drunk," he would want to have sex. I wanted to tell him to take a flying leap. In Al-Anon, however, I had learned that instead of automatically reacting, I could consider my choices. I could (A) refuse angrily, (B) refuse politely, (C) have sex with him as if I were a zombie, or (D) set aside the anger I felt towards the part of him that was being influenced by the disease and instead make love with the sweetheart who somehow survived within the disease. By choosing (A) or (C) I might temporarily feel superior, but the backlash would be feeling ashamed of myself. By choosing (B), I could retain my dignity and continue living with my unrequited sexual desires. By choosing (D), I could perhaps contribute to the healing of our disease-scarred relationship and receive some sexual satisfaction for myself. When I chose (D), I made sure to ask myself if I felt comfortable. If so, then I went for it!

Changing My Behavior

When I was a child and didn't get my way with friends or family, I would have a temper tantrum—little verbal jabs and digs that would hurt—until I got others to give in or fight back. Then I would feel very sorry for myself. This carried over into my adult life, if I could be called "adult" before I came into Al-Anon.

At first my husband tolerated my verbal abuse, so I kept it up. I learned to provoke him without saying a word, with my eyes and with body language. Eventually, he began to fight back—with his fists. I'm not condoning his behavior—physical abuse is simply unacceptable—but I do have to take responsibility for the part I played.

After I came into Al-Anon and heard the suggestion to "Think" before I spoke, things got better. I put a smile on my face. It wasn't in my heart, but it was on my face. I got a Sponsor, who helped me to realize that provocation, on the part of either a drinker or a non-drinker, can be a symptom of the family disease of alcoholism. I had to realize that what I was doing was wrong and be willing to change myself. I also had to learn that he had a disease and I could not change him.

I stopped mentioning my husband's drinking. At first my husband still tried to provoke me, but he didn't hit me. Sometimes when I could think of nothing else to say, I would tell him that I loved him, which was true. This helped both of us to put things in perspective. My husband only lived one month after I came into the program, but in that month I did come to love him more and in a healthier way than I ever had before.

I will be forever grateful to the Al-Anon program for helping me to allow my husband to live his last month in peace. I have married again recently, and so far I have not had the urge to provoke violence from my mate or anyone else. I feel that as long as I continue in Al-Anon and practice the Steps, I won't have to react to that insane urge to hurt or be hurt.

Making Difficult Decisions

My husband's crises became more severe every day. I did as much as possible to keep things "normal" at home, but there were things I couldn't ignore anymore. His alcoholic behavior was affecting my children and myself physically, mentally, and morally. I had to practice the most painful "First Things First" of my life: with the support of my Al-Anon group and the love of God, I decided to leave him.

To his family, I was the rat leaving the ship at the time of disaster. I was the one breaking the promise of staying "in sickness and in health." I have to admit my sense of guilt increased, but after some time, the magic of Al-Anon made me understand that although the separation was painful, I should be realistic: it was better to have three of us alive than dead. I couldn't ask his family to understand the disease of alcoholism; they didn't have a program and I did.

I was full of fear. The only things I knew how to do were to take care of my children and be an Al-Anon member. Since I needed a job and the Al-Anon General Service Office needed somebody to serve, I started working there. I forced myself to concentrate on the sunny side of life and on those good moments I had lived. My desperation decreased, and I realized my blessings were many.

I tried to fill the void in my life with things within

my reach—my children, my Al-Anon group, my studies, books, and so on. But I learned that my external circumstances are not the source of happiness in my life. My happiness comes from within.

After three years, my husband and I are back on the road we started on together several years ago. God acts slowly, but He is always on time.

To anyone else going through a separation, I want to share some of what I learned. I am able to do so because of the clarity that came from working the Al-Anon program. First, I learned to consider myself as a human being, not a robot. Second, although I tried to stay serene, there have been moments of deep loneliness, fear, and tiredness. Third, I had to learn to forgive myself, accept myself, and keep going forward.

Learning about Living

When someone you are just getting to know in Al-Anon dies, it is a sad experience, and Peter's death touched me deeply. I wish I could have said goodbye the last time I spoke with him. I wish I could have told him how much I enjoyed his friendship, but I didn't and now I can't. I learned more about living from his untimely death. I learned about how precious life is and how precious friendships and loved ones are. I, too, have conflict and I have decisions I need to make. The Suggested Al-Anon/Alateen Welcome mentions "placing our problem in its true perspective." This experience has helped me do that. It just seems fruitless not to enjoy life more and experience the special moments that happen each day.

I need to trust that the future will be okay. I'll be all right, even though I'm not sure of the path my life will take. I know that I am on the right path now. I need to trust that my Higher Power will be there for me each day, "One Day at a Time," and will help me make the correct decisions when the time comes. Most of all, I need to be more patient—a virtue that is really difficult for me—and I need to be more grateful for everything that I have.

Your death really taught me a lot, Peter. I'll miss you.

CHAPTER NINE

Practicing these Principles:
Steps Eight and Nine

The family disease of alcoholism thrives on maintaining the status quo. Change is generally unwelcome. Healthy change is a threat. Whenever we take action on our own behalf—when we ignore the nagging voice of the disease that says, "Don't make any trouble!"—we upset the changeless atmosphere in which this family illness most easily flourishes. Whether we take an hour away from our pressing problems to nurture ourselves, choose to step back and allow someone we love to continue moving toward a crisis without our interference, or break an old behavior pattern that no longer works, we are creating new possibilities. Like antiseptic on an open wound, we may feel the sting for a little while after we make such choices. Some of us may find ourselves suddenly full of doubt, though we had been so certain of our decisions. We may become obsessed with the results of actions taken, wondering what everyone will think. Others might feel exhausted, depressed, insecure, or just plain terrible.

When we acknowledge the risks we've taken by making a decision and recognize the progress we've made, our self-esteem receives a powerful boost. Whether we have confronted fear, made a difficult phone call, or initiated a major effort toward changing our lives, we have done what we set out to do. It is up to us to celebrate our victories, even the small ones. We can remember to practice gratitude. When belief in ourselves and in our Higher Power may be the most shaky, our smallest triumphs can help reinforce our faith.

We can't truly know in advance how a difficult situation will affect our lives or the lives of those we love. Persistent searching for the "right" steps to take or the "right" time to take them can tempt us to judge "success" or "failure" by the results of our efforts. We learn in Al-Anon that after careful consideration we can take the action and let go of the results. If we make a decision, and then act on that decision, we have succeeded, whether the results are disappointing or encouraging. Regardless of the outcome, we have done our part. The rest is up to God.

However, just as it is critical to acknowledge the asset side of action-taking, we must also acknowledge the liabilities. Whether we have made carefully considered choices that feel absolutely right for us or have acted impulsively out of fear or anger, our actions have consequences. Sometimes other people get hurt. By taking Step Eight, we acknowledge this fact and become willing to make amends. With this Step we sort out our part, taking responsibility for our actions but also releasing ourselves—and possibly others—from the burden of falsely-held responsibilities. With help from our Higher Power, we find the method of making amends that will allow us to feel that we have done our part. Then we can let go of these past actions by taking the Ninth Step.

We need not judge or punish ourselves, nor justify our behavior or motives. In fact, we take Steps Eight and Nine for our own comfort and well-being, moving ever closer to the God of our understanding.

As with other actions, some of us try to make amends long before we truly understand their purpose. Rather than obtaining freedom, we subject ourselves to frustration, confusion, a sense of failure, or even abuse. Others try never to think about these Steps at all, leaving guilt, resentment, and fear to fester beneath the surface. It is up to each of us to discover the time and method of making amends that are right for us.

Many times, situations we face in recovery parallel those we have confronted before. They offer us an opportunity to choose differently, with greater awareness and understanding, than we have in the past. With Steps Eight and Nine we have a chance to practice being the kind of people we want to be. We who came to Al-Anon with wounded relationships can begin to let go of how everyone else should treat us. Instead we can focus on ourselves and how we behave towards others. We learn to relate to others in a new way. We take responsibility for our part in creating healthy, healing relationships by clearing out the debris that remains from our past behavior. Many of us find that as we practice treating others fairly with love and respect, we ourselves become magnets for love and respect. We can choose to behave with personal integrity, not because it will make someone else feel better, but because it reflects a way of living that enriches and heals us.

Reflecting on Practicing these Principles

When Direct Amends Aren't Possible

When my son died ten years ago at the age of 12 after a truck ran into him and his bicycle, I vowed to be a better person. I felt God chose me to suffer this experience so that I would learn and grow from the pain. To some people this may sound odd, perhaps even deranged, but I needed to hold onto this idea in order to save my sanity.

My guilt was overpowering. I remembered every slap I had administered, every angry word that had poured forth when he misbehaved. He had suffered greatly from my behavior, which had not fully corrected itself even with many years of Al-Anon. I had just begun to make amends to myself and my children when his life was taken from him.

So I set out on the long hard road of working out my grief and trying to find some way to make amends to him. It wasn't easy because I always felt amends had to be made directly. In this case it was not possible. This led to my resolve to offer to help others. When I saw members of my Al-Anon group acting coldly or harshly to their children, I often shared how important it was for me to work on my behavior. I pointed out how difficult it might be to make amends later on. I was also fortunate in holding a job that placed me in a position to reach out to others who were hurting and who needed a soft touch and a gentle hug to ease the pain. After a number of years, I was able to include my son's death in my Al-Anon story. I couldn't handle this the first few years because I would feel as though I were going to pass out. Everything would grow black before me.

I take great comfort in the knowledge that our children are given to us on loan. They are not our possessions. When it is time for them to leave, we must allow them to go. I sometimes forget this with my daughter, because my fear forces me to hold her back and prevent her from doing the things other children always do. This fear, unconscious as it may be, has had a strong influence on her total dependency on my husband and me. She still has difficulty stepping forward and being her own person. Here too, I'm slowly learning that she is only on loan and I must allow her to become an adult.

Aftereffects of Positive Action

Before I became a member of Al-Anon, I not only had no idea how to take actions for myself, I didn't even see any reason why I should. I grew up in an alcoholic household and didn't think I deserved love or happiness. The phrase, "Let us love you until you learn to love yourself," proved to be one of the most important tools in my recovery. As I started to truly love myself, I began to feel that I deserved to take positive actions in my life. In taking more and more of these steps forward, it was hard for me to believe that I had ever lived any other way.

However, after taking positive actions for myself, I often experience uncomfortable aftereffects, which I call "backlash." Just as I began to take good care of myself, this backlash struck. I felt as if I had no recovery and that I had been ridiculous to even think for a second that I could do anything good for myself.

Although it occurs less and less frequently, backlash continues to arise when I take positive actions for myself. I consider it one of the effects alcoholism has had on my life. In Al-Anon I have learned to deal with it in various ways:

I remind myself that this "voice" is my disease and that whatever it has to say is a lie.

Calling an Al-Anon friend will almost always set me on track.

Going to an Al-Anon meeting, where I can hear others sharing their strength, hope, and experience, enables me to remember that, although I am getting better, the stronger I get, the sneakier the disease gets.

Now that I understand more about how the disease works, I am learning to just accept this backlash rather than fight it and give it so much power.

Behaving with Dignity

Whenever I react to unacceptable behavior or to a frightening situation, I give my dignity away. This is one of the things that bothered me so in the past: that I was the person who others took notice of and labeled as "crazy" or "mean," not the alcoholic. To walk away now without making a fool of myself is such a joy. Because of

Al-Anon, I now know that I can stop and think or talk to my Sponsor before I decide what to do or *not* do. Most of the time, when difficult situations arise, I remind myself that my ultimate goal is not to win or be proven right. It is to maintain my dignity and to feel pride in knowing that I won't have to make amends as result of my behavior.

Making Amends

In Step Eight I returned to my Fourth Step inventory and listed the people I had harmed, whether intentionally or unintentionally. Whether or not I decided to take any action was the next part—Step Nine. My Al-Anon recovery had shown me that my conscience would not rest until I cleared away the heartaches of my past. I wrote letters to people who were too far away and explained that I had come to see the error of my ways. I said that I felt I had caused hurt feelings or unhappiness for which I was truly sorry. That was all I had to do. I didn't have to beg their forgiveness or try to get together. I went to others personally—but not until I had asked for guidance to do God's will and for the strength to go ahead. I had to remind myself to expect nothing in return. In fact they could even reject my efforts, and if they did I had no control over that. From most, I received forgiveness and renewed friendships; from others I only received a nod or the word "fine." Once, when I *expected* results, the person changed the subject. I felt shunned until my Sponsor pointed out that I was expecting to achieve my will, not God's.

New Ways to Take Action

After some time in Al-Anon I was fired from my job. In my alcoholic family I had been taught to take whatever job offer came along first, or to pursue work oriented to my unrealistic fantasies (positions I wasn't qualified for or lacked the skills to perform). Al-Anon has helped me learn that it's more important to find out what my needs really are. I can be realistic about my financial needs. I may not need to make as much money as I think I'm worth, or as little as I used to make. My emotional needs include being verbal, so it was important to find a job in which I would have communication with other people. My spiritual needs include having a work environment that is quiet, warm, kind, and gentle, where I can express my feelings openly and freely when appropriate. I need to be around people who allow me to be who I am. Today my self-worth is not based on other people's ability to meet my needs, only on my ability to ask to have my needs met.

Once I had found what my needs were, I took the first three Steps. I recognized my powerlessness: the old way of looking for work made my life unmanageable, and something new had to be done. I had to have the courage to share with people who have known me for years in Al-Anon meetings that I was unemployed again. Otherwise I was not making it real. I already believed, so every morning I got up and said, "I'm willing to work today, God. If that is your will, please show me where."

In the past, when looking for work, I had many job interviews, but this time I was only asked to leave applications. That frightened me until my Sponsor reminded me that I had asked to have things done differently. So I continued to do the footwork for jobs that looked like they had the potential to meet my needs. I understood that whether I got an interview or not, I was still loved. I was the same loving, willing person who had asked for guidance that morning.

One of the most frustrating things during this process was thinking that I was close to a job offer, only to be rejected for no apparent reason. My old behavior would have been to ask for specific reasons for the rejection. Now I simply acknowledged that this was not a place where my Higher Power wanted me to work and that my unique and special abilities were not needed in that place.

There came a point, several months into this process, at which I became frustrated and unwilling, and I stopped doing the Third Step. I decided because of outside financial pressures that I needed to do something *today*. My Higher Power responded by giving me opportunities to meet my financial needs on a temporary basis, but not my emotional and spiritual needs, which are more long-term. Once I realized that I was not going to be abandoned, I got back into the habit of taking the Third Step every day—and on a much more accepting level.

The following week I had four or five interviews. My old behavior in a job interview was to lie about my education, my previous dependability in showing up for work, or my skills. In short, I said yes to everything, which would often land me in a job for which I was either under-qualified or overqualified and leave me feeling guilty. Just as I had done in the alcoholic household, I would find myself manipulating, covering up one lie with another, trying to be as general as possible, and at the same time saying what I thought the person in charge wanted to hear.

The old way does not work any more. My new behavior, learned by working the Al-Anon program, requires doing the footwork, telling the truth, and letting go of the results.

The interviews resulted in three job offers. Two of these were the sort of work I had performed before, which did not meet my financial, emotional, or spiritual needs. However the third one did. After discussing it with my Al-Anon friends, I accepted this job.

The fact that I took this job does not mean that the process has ended. I still have to verbally do Steps One through Three. I ask what my options are, discuss my needs with my Higher Power and others, and accept the results of letting my needs be known.

Asking for What I Need

I was in the worst depression since being divorced, so I decided to call somebody in Al-Anon. When the person said, "How are you?" I was truthful. "I'm not in a good place, "I said. "In fact, I seem to have slipped into a depression and can't seem to climb out." This person replied, "Well, practice what you preach," and went on to discuss something else.

Thinking that I had reached out to the wrong person, I tried again. And again. And again. I heard, "Well, go to meetings and call your Sponsor," and, "You already know how to do depression. Why don't you practice something else?"

I was angry and hurt for days. In alcoholic situations of the past, I had learned it was best to keep my mouth shut when I was hurt. In Al-Anon, I have learned that when I don't communicate, I often get resentful. I start to think I am owed amends. When I blame someone else for the way I feel, I am probably avoiding facing my own responsibilities.

Finally I called each person back and said, "You remember the other day when I tried to talk with you about being depressed? I was in pain and reaching out to you, but you did not hear me. Our friendship is important to me, and you are one of the people whom I need to hear me!" I really did. I was astonished that I could do it, and they were astonished that I did. Their answers were not unanimous acceptance, much less approval. One said, "It scares me when you're not all right," and another said, "I cannot handle it when you are in pain," but we talked it through. In each case the person said, in effect, "Regardless of my reaction, I hope you will call again when you are hurting."

If I feel unheard and I do not let the person know how I feel, I will continue to be unheard. It is up to me to take this action. If I let the person know how I feel and nothing changes, I will find someone who *can* really hear me, who isn't threatened by my pain. I must make sure that I, in turn, listen carefully so that I do not brush off someone who needs to have me listen.

Coming to Terms with Violence

I can remember a dazed, "seeing stars" feeling while being hit about the head by my alcoholic father. I felt anger at the injustice and humiliation and a sense of utter frustration that whatever I did was useless. I remember holding my body stiff and trying not to be aware of his presence when he tried to make up.

I became a very violent person, first at school and then with my husband. He did not come from a violent home, and I think he was horrified by my temper. At the time I interpreted his not hitting me back as rejection. I have also been violent with my daughter, and I usually feel very anxious and guilty about my behavior towards her.

I get immense help from Al-Anon in coming to terms with the violence. I find that sharing at meetings or writing my feelings down is extremely helpful, because then I'm not denying it anymore. The more I look at my own behavior, the less I judge my dad. As I truly accept what has happened and accept myself as I am, I become better able to behave in a peaceful, loving way.

The violence with my daughter is slowly resolving itself. I did turn for help to an outside agency, and I go to counseling once a week. This complements my Al-Anon program and is in no way a substitute. The solutions are surprisingly easy and logical but were quite beyond me. It was suggested that I try to treat my daughter as if she was three rather than six. This has taken much pressure off of both of us and gives her a chance to learn to trust me. She can only go by her own experience with me, and that has not been a good one. Slowly, "One Day at a Time," I try to make amends by being consistent.

Mending Myself

I think the word "amends" means to mend or repair relationships. I also think of mending myself, my broken feelings, and freeing my own conscience. At one time I thought that making amends would be to apologize, but I was brought up apologizing whether I meant it or not. Today I look at apologizing as merely one method of making amends.

Making amends is not a punishment for me. My experience in Al-Anon has confirmed that atonement need not be painful or unpleasant. There was a time when I felt that I needed to punish myself to make up for my wrongs, but I discovered that this was merely adding to the wrongs I had already done to myself.

This Step is for *my* peace of mind. If others receive satisfaction from my amends, that is great. My amends do not depend on someone else's forgiveness. I need to forgive myself.

Dealing with the Past

As I began to recover in Al-Anon from the effects of another's alcoholism, I saw that I not only had much work to do on myself, but I also had amends to make to my two girls. I felt I could best make amends by stepping out of their lives completely and letting them live with someone who could be a mother in the real sense of the word. Later the social workers involved felt it would be a good idea if I would step back into the picture to help them deal with the past. I agreed to do so, for this would be another aspect of Steps Eight and Nine. I saw them just a few days ago, and I was overwhelmed by how beautiful they really are. I told them my story in detail, emphasizing something we learn over and over again in Al-Anon: one of the hardest tasks we will ever be assigned is letting go of the past.

Backlash

For me, some kind of backlash or negative reaction usually follows an action, thought, or word that is in my best interest—something self-loving. The action may be small—speaking up for myself by stating what I think or want—or it may be grand—landing a wonderful job or realizing one of my dreams. One of the most powerful experiences of backlash I can remember began simply enough with a phone call from my mother to let me know she had bought an airline ticket to visit me. Now, in my family, the "family" is all-important. Loyalty, respect, obedience, oneness of feelings and thoughts—these are taken for granted like the air we breathe. Nevertheless, I said to my mother, "It would be a good idea, Mom, for us to talk about dates and schedules before you buy a ticket." That was it. One simple remark, followed by a long, painful pause.

I felt as if I had killed her, that I had committed the worst sin in the book merely because I expressed a desire.

We decided to think about it and talk later. After we hung up, I proceeded to get so sick to my stomach, so terrified, and so frantic, I didn't know what to do or say. I was falling, falling, and I couldn't stop. Thank God, my recovering husband and my Al-Anon support system were there.

My mother and I had three phone calls that night, each one trying to clarify and communicate, to separate love from disease. Before Al-Anon I would have done anything she wanted and bent myself any which way to please her. Even in recovery, I might have fallen to pieces had I not realized that feelings aren't facts and that I had done nothing wrong no matter how I felt. My Sponsor and program friends helped me to keep in mind that my actions were adult, responsible, and good for me.

Backlash can hinder my success, but it is something the Al-Anon program and my dear friends in it are helping me to recognize and to heal from. I wouldn't have even thought of speaking up, had it not been for Al-Anon and the recovery I had worked hard for and been blessed with. It was the beginning of a change in my relationship with my mother that continues to this day.

Standing by My Decisions

When my son was about 20, he took his first drink. From then on, I believe, he was an alcoholic drinker. Naturally, being his mother, I was very upset. I tried reasoning with him, offering enticements and bribes—everything I could think of doing. Getting him to stop drinking seemed like the most important thing in my life. Months slipped by, then years, and suddenly he was 30 and I was miserable.

I had been told on numerous occasions about Al-Anon, but I was too embarrassed to admit that my son had a problem I couldn't cure. Eventually I allowed myself to be dragged to an Al-Anon meeting. Right from the beginning, I loved it! Everything people said made sense. I got a Sponsor at my first meeting and went home so excited that I couldn't sleep. I immediately started going to daily meetings and putting into practice the things I learned there.

I would have thought my son would be pleased with my changed behavior. He had always complained about my nagging. With the help of Al-Anon, I stopped nagging. He had hated the way I always stuck my nose into his life, tried to fix messes, and made critical remarks about his friends. Believe it or not, after two months with me minding my own business, my son gave me an ultimatum—either I stopped going to Al-Anon ("the cult," he called it) or he would begin proceedings to have me declared incompetent. His reaction was such a shock that I did not believe him. Angrily, I told him to go live his own life and I would live mine.

Eventually I found myself in a court of law, having to explain to the judge why I wanted to live my own life and what "the cult" had done to give me back my self-respect. After dismissing the case, the judge suggested to my son that he might want to give some thought to getting his own life together.

My son's reactions were and still are angry and abusive. I have let him know that I still care for him but will not allow myself to be mistreated. At this time we are at a standstill. I have learned that things change when my Higher Power is ready but not always when I am. Throughout this experience, my Al-Anon friends have stood by me, never telling me what to do but supporting my decisions to live the way I feel is best for me.

Making Amends to My Child

Before I found Al-Anon, I literally used my son as a "whipping boy." He was so young and in no way capable of defending himself. I can remember him curled up in the corner of the couch, too scared to move and too confused to understand all that was happening to him. There was no way he could escape this terrible ordeal because I would not allow him to stay with anyone else. No one was going to tell me how to handle my child.

He was finally spared any further abuse when God guided me to Al-Anon and my wife to AA. We are both working our programs to the best of our ability. My son? He is also growing in Alateen. The love that has grown between us is beautiful.

I have a lot of amends to make to my son. I will do it "One Day at a Time" by listening to him, trying to understand him, and just plain talking to him. I realize he is a human being and must first live as a child and do childish things. I am working with him as a father but also as a friend.

My heart goes out to parents who see their children suffer through the terrors of the disease of alcoholism.

Have faith and trust in your Higher Power. These words may seem hollow. They did to me at one time. Now I turn to God every day and thank Him for delivering us all from that living nightmare.

Resentment and Amends

I loved my husband and now he was going to leave me for another woman. He was my god, my obsession. How could that woman do this to me? How would I raise my five children? Even though I was in Al-Anon, fear immobilized me and I kept asking myself questions that had no answers—what-if's, but's, how's, and why's. I had nightmares frequently, in which I beat up this other woman and pulled out her hair. I would wake up drenched with perspiration and during this time lost 30 pounds. When I saw her I maliciously gave her verbal abuse. I even involved my children in this sick behavior, turning them against their father, who loved them dearly. Anger, hate, and resentment—all part of the family disease of alcoholism—were killing me.

Working through the Twelve Steps, I became aware that I had not completed Steps Eight and Nine. It was easy for me to justify not making direct amends, but I knew it was something that I had to do for total serenity and forgiveness. I heard in an Al-Anon meeting that we must pray for the willingness to be willing. It finally came, though it took a long time. One helpful suggestion was to pray daily for the person I resented, even if I didn't want to, asking that God grant them everything I wanted in my life, like serenity, happiness, and security.

Hard to do? You bet!

One evening a thought came to me, "Call her." Chills came over me, accompanied by a sleepless night. The following morning I humbly got to my knees and asked God to help me. I made the call, placing the focus on me and how I had wronged her. I asked if she would accept amends for the way I treated her in the past. I told her that my pride was hurt, that I was filled with anger and resentments, and that I felt she was a threat to me. There was a silence, followed by, "I'm sorry too; I wanted to make amends also, but could not." We chatted about our feelings and about the children. When the conversation was finished, I returned to my knees, thanking God and weeping with relief.

Today I can work with her at community functions with calmness. God gave me the perfect opportunity to tell my husband and children individually. All had the same reaction of disbelief, shock, and tears—evidence of happiness that "it was over." To me this is the greatest miracle that I have experience working through the Twelve Steps of Al-Anon recovery and observing God doing for me what I could not do for myself.

Part Four

Moving On

CHAPTER TEN

Love and Forgiveness:
Steps Ten, Eleven, and Twelve

Al-Anon is a program of hope. It shows us a way to become students of life on life's terms: we start to recognize the opportunities for growth hidden within every situation. We learn that it is possible to find serenity within ourselves, even when surrounded by chaos. As an old Chinese proverb observes, "If I keep a green bough in my heart, the singing bird will come."

Still, it is easy to become discouraged. Many of us find ourselves grappling again and again with issues we thought we had overcome long ago. We sometimes doubt that we are making any progress at all. One member likens this aspect of the recovery process to climbing a spiral staircase: while it may seem we are getting nowhere, going in circles, we actually revisit old issues from an ever-high vantage point. As we practice Steps Ten, Eleven, and Twelve, we become less likely to invalidate the Al-Anon recovery we have already achieved. We learn that there is life after crisis, and that, with the help of these Steps, we can move on. Most of us find that the quality of our lives continues to improve as we apply the Al-Anon program not only to crisis situations but to our everyday lives.

Step Ten helps us to live consciously, in the present,

by continuing to take personal inventory, acknowledging our gains and our gratitude, promptly admitting when we are wrong. No longer must we accumulate burdens of guilt or resentment that will become heavier and more potent over time. Each day, each new moment can be an opportunity to clear the air, to start again, fresh and free.

The Eleventh Step can be the means for filling the terrible, aching void that so many of us experience within. Having tried to fill this emptiness with practically everything—sweets, relationships, rage, shopping, overwork—and having failed to find lasting relief, we can turn to meditation for a solution. Unlike these other sources of comfort, meditation fills us up from the inside out and leaves us a little more whole each time. The search for the particular form of meditation that best suits us, whether formal or informal, can be part of our striving for a deeper relationship with the God of our understanding.

Prayer offers another way to improve our conscious contact with our Higher Power. Most of us have prayed for everything but God's will at one time or another. Some of us got what we requested but found that it didn't make us as happy as we had expected, or that it wasn't enough. Others felt that our prayers had gone unanswered when we didn't get what we wanted. The humility that results from working the previous Steps reminds us that we don't always have the perspective to know what is best for us. So when we work the Eleventh Step, we ask only for "knowledge of God's will for us, and the power to carry it out." Power here does not always mean strength, determination, or force; it may take the form of gentleness, willingness to bend, or surrender to God's will.

Step Twelve states that the result of working these Steps is a spiritual awakening. Some experience this as a sudden, life-changing revelation, while others sense a more subtle, gradual spiritual evolution. The Twelfth Step goes on to explain that the principles which led to this awakening can apply to any situation confronting us. Others in similar situations may also benefit from the experience, strength, and hope we gain by practicing these principles in all our affairs. Yet it is not simply for the sake of others that we need to share these experiences and thereby carry the message. There is no better way to keep our spiritual benefits than by giving them away with love, free of expectations, and with no strings attached. Giving away material goods depletes our supply (if I give you half my lunch, I will have less than before). When we give away what we have received in Al-Anon, most of us get back far more than we give.

Our responses to difficult situations can move us toward becoming more fully the men and women we are capable of being or they can leave us feeling like victims. It's up to us. Even the darkest of moments can be faced with a grateful heart, if not for the crisis itself, at least for the growth it can evoke with the help of our Higher Power. We may not be free to choose the substance of the lessons we will learn, but we can choose whether the experience will leave us more cautious, defensive, hard, frightened, and rigid, or more flexible, faith-filled, and available to life.

Forgiveness can sometimes make the difference. Unfortunately, forgiveness is often confused with judgment: I will examine the ways in which I feel you have injured me and find you guilty. Then, out of my generous, spiritual heart, I will condescend to absolve you of guilt. This is not forgiveness, but arrogance. If we have judged, forgiveness can be the means by which our minds are returned to humility—and thereby to real freedom: we can remember that we are in no position to rule on the worthiness of another. Every person, simply by being a child of God, is worthy of love and respect. By shifting the focus from the other person's "wrongs" to our own, we can take responsibility for having expressed condemnation. Then we can forgive ourselves. We are human. We sometimes make mistakes and may have to make amends for our behavior. Nevertheless, we have no more right to condemn ourselves than to condemn others. We deserve to treat ourselves with honestly and love.

Many of us who have been affected by the disease of alcoholism find that love and pain can easily become interlinked, especially when we face a difficult situation. Creativity often seems to dry up, along with our warmth and trust for others and our willingness to care. We may feel old, cold, and barren, and doubt that we will ever feel enthusiasm or vitality again. Recovery in Al-Anon can free us from despair. We move from being at the mercy of any problem that comes along to an inner certainty that no matter what happens in our lives, we will be able to face it, deal with it, and learn from it with the help of our Higher Power. Like the movement of a glacier, we may not recognize our progress right away, but the effects of working the Al-Anon program are profound and lasting. No matter how hopeless we may feel in response to personal tragedy, there is every reason to hope. So very many of us have not only survived similar events but have flourished. The miracle of recovery is that no matter what circumstances we must face, we are able to live and love once more.

Reflections on Love and Forgiveness

Growing and Healing

My husband was physically abusive, first with me and eventually with our two children. I always forgave him because I "understood" him. I knew he didn't want to act that way. In time, I became less forgiving, more hurt, and more angry until I, too, became a child abuser. I justified my behavior by comparing it to his: my behavior wasn't quite as violent. But my guilt and shame in turn fostered the acceptance of his abuse. After all, I felt, I deserved to be punished. Eventually my son sexually abused my daughter. I remember once, when my daughter timidly tried to tell me about it, my pitiful, inadequate advice to her was, "Stay away from him." I remember thinking, "If his father finds out, he'll kill him." My overwhelming, paralyzing guilt, fear, and shame—my immense denial—contributed to our family's downward spiral into deeper and deeper levels of suffering from alcoholism.

By the grace of God, about seven years ago we found AA, Al-Anon, and Alateen. We didn't get sick overnight, and we weren't "cured" immediately; recovery is a long-term, ongoing process. I went to a great many meetings and actually listened, instead of feeling sorry for myself and telling people that they didn't understand. After a while I was able to ask for hugs and accept them from people who seemed to genuinely care about me and my feelings. I didn't share many of our secrets and nightmares for quite a while, but I began to believe that a better life was possible through Al-Anon and that we deserved that better life.

By the time I got a Sponsor I was ready to use one. I spent hours and hours talking with her because she really understood how I felt and listened to me without judging or blaming. She introduced me to the Higher Power I had heard about at meetings. She told me that God would forgive me and show me how to forgive myself.

I stopped trying to win arguments with my husband and kids. I finally figured out that a fight involving three people was worse than a fight between two, and that nobody could fight by themselves. I stopped adding fuel to the fire by seeing I had choices, one of which was to mind my own business. I learned to stop insisting I was right, and to be humble enough to call my Sponsor.

When my two children began using drugs and alcohol, I was truly grateful that Al-Anon had taught me to take care of myself. They went through the courts, foster homes, and runaway shelters until they finally found their places in the AA program. Their cries taught me to detach with love and to lean on the love and support of the program and my Al-Anon friends. The Twelve Steps provided a plan of action that was clear-cut and gradual and offered the healing spiritual direction we all needed.

I am still married to that same handsome, charming, now recovering alcoholic. We are more in love than ever. Our lives aren't perfect and neither are we. But today we have a marriage that is a growing partnership. Our relationship takes work, and we're worth it! Today I am safe and happy and I feel free. I owe it all to my Higher Power and Al-Anon.

Accepting Unconditional Love

As I got into recovery in Al-Anon and began to concentrate on letting go and letting God, I reached a point of spiritual crisis. The loving God I kept hearing about in meetings and reading about in Al-Anon literature was not a God I knew. Out of my pain and confusion I realized I had been living with an unhealthy concept of God. For 20 years I had believed I had a good spiritual life. I taught Sunday school, led Bible studies, and went to church every Sunday. I was going to find the right way to live and not make any mistakes.

When I realized how much of my life was taken up with pleasing others, I realized I was also trying to please God. I knew God loved me but didn't really believe it was unconditional. I felt I had a responsibility to love God back and do what he wanted. Now I believe that He stands with me through whatever choices I make. He loves me as I make mistakes and make amends. With His help my life can blossom in a way it never has before.

Building a New Life

A life crisis and the grace of God led me to Al-Anon. The program taught me to love and value myself, and gradually I came to believe that I did not have to allow another person to physically abuse me. Although my spouse had left our home, we still had a relationship that included violence and threats of violence. With the help of the Al-Anon program, I was able to take steps to protect myself both legally and physically. At the same time, I held out a hand to my spouse, suggesting we go for help to repair our marriage and to learn constructive, nonviolent ways of communication. My single stipulation was that there be no further violence.

The alcoholic's reply was, "Violence? I've never been violent to you." This was followed by a threatening telephone call.

My dream of a new start and a marriage with positive, healthy interaction was not meant to be. My spouse did not wish to continue our marriage, and I was left to grieve the loss of a dream that never was and never could be. Again, the support of fellow Al-Anon members and the growth I was making through the program, especially my increased faith in a Higher Power, helped me to continue building a new life. Through the Fourth and Fifth Steps, I was able to look at the violence, accept it for what is was, and see the part my own illness played in it.

I never would have chosen to learn my lessons through such a trying situation, but with the support of my Al-Anon friends and the miracle of the Steps, I have been able to replace my fear with faith, my guilt with understanding, and my bitterness and anger with acceptance. My growth has been painful but rewarding. Living with violence left emotional scars that cannot be erased overnight. Today I know that I am recovering a day at a time from the effects of alcoholism on my life. With the help of my Higher Power and the Al-Anon program, I never have to allow such violence to be a part of my life again.

Learning to Forgive

My memories of my parents' drinking involve yelling, cursing, and then physical violence. Consequently, I was the "good little girl," always trying, always behaving properly—so that I wouldn't cause trouble. Extreme anger, even my own, has always frightened me, but I am dealing with it through Al-Anon.

My memories of the incest with my father have always been foggy. It happened during my early and mid-teens. He would come to my room in the middle of the night, and I would awaken after he had begun to fondle me. I would pretend to remain asleep, but I remember enjoying the physical sensation even though I knew it was wrong. Now I know that the physical response was natural, but at the time I felt terrible guilt.

I never remember hating him. In many other ways he was a kind, gentle, loving father. I have had to deal with more anger, hostility, and hate for my mom than my dad.

I had never told anyone until I told my fiancé. Through the grace of God, he listened to my story, accepted, loved, and comforted me, and he did not judge my father. Because he made it easier for me to heal, I will be forever grateful to him. It surprises me that sexually I seem to be okay. Despite all that I have read to the contrary about the effects of incest, my husband and I have a good sex life that I thoroughly enjoy.

I have survived—without hate and with a loving, full life. Because of all I have learned in Al-Anon, I now know how sick my dad was to do what he did. I am a parent myself, and I know that I would never willingly hurt my kids. In my disease I did hurt them in spite of my love for them. I believe the same is true of my father.

Facing Facts and Moving On

Bankruptcy. The word itself implies failure and shame to me. I was raised in a strict, ethnic home where I learned the value of hard work and financial responsibility. How could I have gotten in this position?

It wasn't just the alcoholic's fault—I was managing the money. Denial takes many forms, and I had been living a fantasy that my husband would soon get a good job and we would get caught up. I twisted Al-Anon's "One Day at a Time" slogan to justify our failure to plan ahead or to live within our means. Budgeting money that you *know* is coming makes sense. Spending money you hope will come tomorrow doesn't.

If the alcoholic had actually gotten a job, we might have been okay. But it was *my* decision to support him, to give in to his (and my) whims, and to keep spending money we didn't have.

Al-Anon encourages me to take responsibility for my choices, but also to forgive myself. After all, I did learn something, and this may have been the only way my

Higher Power could get my attention to teach it.

Bankruptcy is no picnic. We will continue to face the consequences in the future, but we don't have to be scarred for life. No one has branded our foreheads to mark us in public. The only people who know are the few program friends who supported us through the whole mess. Life goes on. Even the supermarket still takes our checks. We no longer avoid our mailbox. With the help and support of our programs, and with a new willingness to face the truth, we have gained control of our financial life. We even have fun! I must share this with everyone: there *is* life after bankruptcy!

A Clean Slate with Step Ten

Under the great strain of a crisis, the Tenth Step helped me to lay out my day in time blocks. I found myself inventorying my morning on the way to work, then discussing it with my Higher Power and working on improving my attitude where needed. Sometimes I needed to stop playing the victim, or stop permitting others to infringe on my rights, or realize when I had offended others. Then I found myself doing inventory at noon, starting my afternoon with a clean slate rather than clinging to old hurts, angers, or resentments. I found that if I go over my workday on the way home, my evening could be approached in a better frame of mind.

Struggling to Forgive

I find forgiveness one of the hardest spiritual concepts to deal with. A part of me wants to cling to old resentments, but I know that the more I forgive, the better my life works.

A big project for me in Al-Anon has been forgiving the guy who had an affair with my lover several years ago during my lover's early sobriety. Mind you, he and I were separated at the time. It's been really hard, though, not to blame the other man for my pain and jealousy.

Al-Anon's three A's (awareness, acceptance, and action) have provided a blueprint. The first step toward forgiving this man has been to simply acknowledge my feelings toward him. I'm frightened of him; he seems to have the power to deprive me of something I treasure—my relationship—and I feel angry. I've written a Fourth Step on this.

Then I try to accept my feelings, which can be tough. Part of me judges them as illogical, not spiritual enough, unrecovered, and unacceptable. However, until I compassionately accept my feelings, they keep me prisoner.

The action part for me begins with prayer and cultivating a willingness to change. I ask God to heal my relationship with this man. I concentrate on the Sixth and Seventh Steps. I realize that the situation parallels my history with my younger brother—I resented *his* appearance too, and felt threatened by it. Separating these "loads of laundry" has relieved some of my resentment.

This experience has shown me how much I still look to other people to be my source of love and sustenance. The more I switch my dependence from my lover to God, the less reason I have to hold a grudge against the other man. He and I have spoken in recent months, sharing some of our feelings and making amends to each other. It's an ongoing process and a deep one.

Changing My Attitude

A year and a half before attending my first Al-Anon meeting, I learned about my husband's incest with my daughter. At that time I played judge and jury over his life—I couldn't have been crueler. Later, when I found myself thinking about it in Al-Anon, I had to ask what I could change, and the answer was: only my attitude. I was able to talk to my wonderful Sponsor about all of it, especially my attitudes. When my husband finally told me that he had been sexually abused by his mother, my heart was at least able to go out to the little boy in him. So, as in all other things, the Al-Anon tools can work with this, too.

Steps Ten, Eleven, and Twelve

I was starting to feel pretty good. I was beginning to trust my Al-Anon recovery. Because of all the work I had done with the Steps and other tools, I had experienced amazing freedom from the effects of another's alcoholism, which had once paralyzed my whole life.

Still, I had to be constantly aware of the inner twinge that told me I was stepping on toes or that one of my old defects was rearing its ugly head again. I didn't want to react to those old emotions as I had in the past. I asked for guidance each morning, read Al-Anon literature, and took time to meditate. If I realized I had harmed someone and did nothing about it, the knot in my stomach grew until I felt so miserable that I had to have a look at what was bothering me. The longer I let these actions go, the harder it became to make amends. So I had to admit my wrongs promptly—the sooner the better.

Prayer and meditation became routine and I would feel the lack whenever I neglected them. I had trouble learning how to meditate. I read a great deal of literature on the subject, and talked to Al-Anon friends. At first, when it still seemed awkward, I had to do something visual, like lighting a candle and watching the flame. I would concentrate on the flame until my mind cleared, then read a beautiful prayer. In prayer I would always try to ask for guidance to do God's will. I would remind myself to "Let Go and Let God," recognizing that only God knows what is best for me, that nothings happens in God's world by mistake, and that I can let Him look after my problems and my family's problems.

Once I looked back over everything that had happened since I started with Step One, I realized there had been many changes and many new feelings that could never have been accomplished on my own. I had certainly had a spiritual awakening. Being able to rely on my Higher Power to help get my life back into focus, to take an honest look at myself, to have the courage to make amends, to see the good and bad about myself and still love myself, to turn my life over to a Higher Power, to relax with prayer and meditation—these were all spiritual awakenings. I had changed! I was no longer the same person. It was all a result of the Steps. I felt compelled to return the giving, the listening, the sharing. I was scared, but I tried talking to a newcomer to Al-Anon, and that was another spiritual awakening. I went on a Twelfth Step call and experienced more new growth. I try to practice these principles in all my affairs: with my family, my job, my friends, and myself. I have found it necessary to go through the Twelve Steps regularly, and I change every time I do.

Opportunities to Learn

When I first found out my husband was having a serious affair, I went into shock. I felt I would surely die if my marriage was over. I was an absolute zombie for three weeks—immobilized, unable to talk to anyone about it, and certainly unable to confront my husband. Finally, I made an appointment with a counselor. She recognized that the main problem was not my husband's infidelity but his alcoholism and its effects on my life. She suggested I go to Al-Anon.

I got involved quickly, chose a Sponsor after my third or fourth meeting, and really worked hard—as hard as I could at the time. The hard work paid off. My marital situation got worse, but I got better in spite of it. My marriage ended in a divorce. The last few months of my marriage were very difficult and the divorce process was extremely painful. Nonetheless, working the Twelve Steps to the best of my ability helped me survive. It helped me to understand that all the events were opportunities for me to learn and were really what was best for me; they were a part of the overall plan the God of my understanding had for me and everyone else concerned. Today I believe God's will for me is to keep in conscious contact with Him and be a happy, loving person who will carry the message to others by trying to be an example of His joy, love, and peace. Today I pray only for knowledge of God's will for me and the power to carry that out.

Giving Up Judgment

I first entered Al-Anon to deal with problems stemming from the alcoholism in my husband's family. After two years of meetings I realized, "Wow, the same patterns existed in my family, but my dad didn't drink that much.

Then, within a short time, my whole life changed, and these realizations were put on hold. I left my husband. I started working, while raising my two children as a single parent. I was also going to therapy to deal with the effects of sexual abuse. And my Sponsor moved out of state. My problems began to torment me night and day. I knew the real problem was me. I attended Al-Anon meetings only sporadically. I was miserable. I longed for the serenity I had once found with Al-Anon's help.

I felt I was in a slip from the Al-Anon program even though I had attended meetings and made phone calls. I realized that I had been reaching out to people who enabled me to dwell on problems rather than solutions. I was getting too many opinions. I needed a Sponsor.

I began to see that there are many ways to recover

from life's tragedies, but Al-Anon is the best way to recover from the effects of alcoholism. For two years I had read many other philosophies, but no Al-Anon literature except my *One Day at a Time in Al-Anon* book. I remembered hearing that Al-Anon Conference Approved Literature was the glue that held our program together. I decided to "Keep It Simple," reading only Al-Anon literature.

I was impatient in meetings because I sometimes heard talk that sounded to me like therapy, not Al-Anon. I had become so resentful that I couldn't appreciate Al-Anon experience, strength, and hope when it was shared. I had to stop judging people, both in and out of meetings. Al-Anon taught me that all people, whether they attend meetings or attend bars, had a Higher Power, and I wasn't it. I learned to take what I liked and leave the rest.

With the help of the program, I discovered that the same merry-go-round, the same anger, denial, and guilt that I later experienced in reaction to my husband's family, had been present in my childhood. I started feeling better, especially when I reached out to members who were serious about their program.

The biggest help I get is from an Al-Anon member listening to me and accepting me, then gently reminding me of a slogan, the Serenity Prayer, or a Step. I also find it useful to hear others share their own experience.

I am still separated from my husband, who is still drinking. My job is difficult, and I continue to have problems due to the sexual abuse. But today, thanks to

Al-Anon, I am okay. I don't need to solve all my problems at one time. I just need to "Let Go and Let God" and enjoy this moment. It's all I've got.

Learning from Loss

My best friend is dying of AIDS. In the past I would have been angry at God for taking my friend away from me. Today I am grateful for the time we have had together to share our love and life with each other. Through my friendship with him I have seen how important it is to live each day to its fullest. I live "One Day at a Time" and I love my life today. I even love the ability to feel sad because my friend is leaving me. Today I can cry about my grief and know that God will give me as much as I can handle, and will take care of me even as I let go of my friend. I am not alone. Today I have God and my Al-Anon program—and myself.

Redefining Love

For the longest time, sex in my life referred to gender, not an act of love between husband and wife. I overreacted to everything, because, as I told my alcoholic husband, I was frustrated. Yet when he did turn towards me, I rejected him unkindly and made remarks that could have made the most potent of men impotent.

I used my frustration as energy—angry energy. I cleaned house like a maniac. Everything had to be my way and I was never satisfied. I know now that all I wanted was to be loved, but without being loving in return. How can any man be loving to a wife who is always berating him and screaming, "Love me!"

Three years ago, my husband joined AA and I joined Al-Anon. Life has gotten better. Our sex life wouldn't compare to that of any of the great lovers, but it is satisfying, loving, and even fun!

Through the Al-Anon program I have become more sure of my own worth and don't feel so lonely and unloved as I did. I have also come to learn that love is an attitude I don't have to prove or have proven to me. My husband had always been an undemonstrative person, and I can accept that now. Al-Anon has helped me know that I don't have to take it personally or try to make him change. Last August was our 30th Anniversary, and we reaffirmed our wedding vows. When I made my vows to him this time, I meant it with all my heart.

Celebrating Life

Four years into my second chaotic, violent, and this time alcoholic marriage, God allowed me to find Al-Anon. How can I tell of the changes that helped me become a willing participant in the grand celebration of life? For now, in spite of a terminal illness, I see each day as a beautiful gift from God. Al-Anon members have taught me the value and joy of life, that true happiness comes from God within me and not from other people or things of this world. God has forgiven me.

Al-Anon and the Twelve Steps have helped me to forgive myself.

The very first time I "worked" the Steps, I did them all in two hours. Now I am happy to admit that sometimes it takes weeks or years for just one of the Steps to be accomplished.

Today my Higher Power is my best friend. When I walk towards Him and even when, in my humanness, I walk away, He is always there with arms outstretched. This is the same way I am greeted at Al-Anon—arms outstretched for a hug or a pat on the back. Al-Anon has allowed me to be me. With this freedom, I have found new pieces of myself. I'm not where I want to be, but thank God and Al-Anon, I'm not where I've been.

Thank you for the support that let me know I was loved when I could not, would not, love myself. Thank you for letting me find out who I am (a child of God) and what I am (a grateful member of Al-Anon). Where am I going? With the help of Al-Anon members and the Steps, wherever God's wisdom directs me. When? Today! "One Day at a Time."

Finding Forgiveness

He had flaunted the other woman in front of our friends and children. I was too numb to face a divorce and go on alone. How grateful I am that, with professional help, I finally made a choice to stay in my marriage. I would have missed being introduced to Al-Anon and the enjoyable five years of sobriety we had before his death.

I thought I had finished with the Eighth and Ninth Steps, but I could not erase the thoughts of "that woman" from my mind. I was still hurting. God kept nudging me. Why? One day a small voice told me I had to forgive myself for all the bad things I was carrying in my mind about "her" and turn them over to Him. I saw that I was willing. In the process I became able to forgive this woman and my husband. I came to realize that I had contributed to the problem by not confronting issues. Had I not enjoyed the role of the hurt wife who was being so good to hold her family together, no matter what? I damaged my children by my attitudes and behavior.

Al-Anon is still my lifeline, and I am grateful to my program friends who insisted that there was a place for me in Al-Anon as a widow. I'll never graduate. At times God still allows part of the pain from my past to surface to be dealt with, but only when I am capable of handling it. This is a program for living, and even as old age creeps in, I feel I can still be of service and continue to grow and learn.

Meeting My Needs with Al-Anon

I always felt that if I could identify a problem and put a label on it, then it was up to me to solve it. I struggled for years in my unhappy marriage, willing to try anything to fix it, to make it happy. My biggest complaint was my husband's lack of support. I looked to him for companionship, conversation, caring about my troubles, sharing my religion, and more.

It came to me slowly but surely that I did have this relationship in my life—with Al-Anon friends. My spiritual journey was being taken with my Sponsor; another Al-Anon friend was willing to listen to my job-related problems and give me input; another shared my grief and my journey to peace when my beloved sister died; I had but to make a phone call and someone would join me for a cup of coffee or a walk in our beautiful nature preserve nearby. I had it all—in different people, but all loving and caring for me. This realization led me to peace, gratitude, and letting go of the demands on my husband to be "everything" for me.

We have sobriety now and the slow building of a relationship, finally, after 35 years of marriage. I pray for patience in its development. I am deeply grateful for each small step forward and for the awareness of that growth.

Replacing Self-Pity with Gratitude

It is not easy to live in an active alcoholic situation, and I am not going to say that I will always stay with it. I try not to say "always" or "never." For the moment I'm trying to postpone saying, "I've had it!" Several longtime Al-Anon members have said, "We can't tell you what to do; you must make your own decision." Meanwhile, what helps me best is focusing on working my program to help *me*. The self-pity that I have been comfortable with for so long needs to be replaced with gratitude. Sure, there are plenty of reasons that I could cry, "Poor me." Instead I am thankful for a much longer list of things. I am learning to thank God each morning for His gift: a beautiful day, no matter what the weather or the problems.

Sometimes I have been tempted to think that the program is just "psyching myself up" so I can live in this difficult situation, but looking over the Steps reminds me that the program is an agreement with God to make the necessary changes in my life. I certainly do not know what is best for my life; I want to do what I can and trust God for the rest.

Benefiting from Painful Experiences

You all taught me long ago that I must not back God into a corner, shake my finger in His face, and demand, "Why me?" You suggest I ask instead, "What am I supposed to understand?" Pain can be valuable if it brings me closer to God.

How, then, do I use my Al-Anon program to help me handle suffering? I go ahead and feel the feeling. I quit covering up. I do not repress the pain. I inventory the situation and talk to someone about it—perhaps several people. It is important that I share with others. It is equally important that I don't belabor my sharing, thereby giving it more energy and attention than it deserves. I must not let myself become obsessed with the current problem, whatever it is. I use the slogans, trite as they may sometimes seem. "How Important Is It?" I ask myself. "Easy Does It." I try to remember that this, too, shall pass.

I thank God for whatever is happening. I can no longer just accept it. So I have thanked Him for all kinds of difficult situations—arthritic pain, migraines, viruses, relationships that ended, financial worries, and career worries. I do not mean that I am glad when a difficulty is happening. I thank Him for the seemingly bad because in the past He has always brought good out of my suffering. When I thank Him, I am telling Him that I have faith that He will do so again.

Things Happen for a Reason

When our alcoholic loved one was in treatment, all of us in the close family circle started learning about Al-Anon and the importance of our own recovery. Our loved one had several relapses after treatment, and I chose to learn all I could for my own recovery. I wanted sanity and serenity whether he did or not. Now I can see why that was necessary. Without the serenity I gained, I could not even begin to cope with life as it is today.

Through Al-Anon I have learned not to interfere with recovery or relapse. There is a reason why things happen as they do. Someday we will find out what that reason is, if we are supposed to know. I guess that applies to my own recovery as well.

My son has temporarily moved back into my home and is living with me as he works his way through recovery. His temper is short, his sleep is erratic, and his patience almost non-existent. If I did not have such a strong commitment to slogans such as "Let Go and Let God," "Live and Let Live," "Just for Today," and "One Day at a Time," I would be totally out of control by now. With my new knowledge of how to live the Al-Anon way, I can accept and love him regardless of his bouts of ill temper. I believe that it was part of the master plan for me to progress in my recovery before he even started his; that way I can live with sobriety.

Restoring My Hope

I feel profoundly that had I not found Al-Anon at the precise moment I did, I would be eternally in a violent alcoholic situation into which my children might have been drawn. I had reached the point where I was without resilience, will, or hope. Had I not then found Al-Anon, I would have been so despairing that I would have given up trying altogether and would have just continued, totally cowed, along the path I was on.

I am grateful for so much. When I came to Al-Anon I heard that no situation was really hopeless, but I thought mine was the exception. I feared that by facing my situation I would lose my husband, my family, everything. Instead, all that I held most dear—husband, children, family life—has been restored to me. I cannot help feeling that my Higher Power put me in this situation—the only situation that would make me seek help. Had my husband not been violent, I would doubtless have continued in my own destructive fashion. The damage, especially to my children, might have become too great to be put right. Al-Anon helped me to make changes within myself. As I began to recover, the whole family was affected. I couldn't have made it happen through the force of my will. Al-Anon has given me the support and the tools I need to live sanely: detachment, Al-Anon phone calls, sponsorship, and all the rest. Al-Anon has given me back my hope.

Finding Hope in Others' Recovery

Having been raised in an alcoholic home, I always felt

that I'd been somehow cheated out of a good life. The other kids I hung around with seemed to have comfortable homes where they were happy. I would rarely invite my friends to my house because I never knew when things might explode. There was a lot of yelling, screaming, and throwing things. I recall feeling scared, lonely, unique, and above all else, quite angry. I would often vent my anger on those around me, fighting with other young boys with little or no provocation at all. As I grew older the fights became more frequent and violent. The anger became rage.

As an adult, I created many difficult situations, but none more difficult than with my children. I have been married three times, and each of these women suffered from the disease of alcoholism. Whenever one of them would do anything that displeased me, though I would not strike my wife, I would beat my children. Again I felt cheated, and somebody was going to pay.

When I finally arrived at an Al-Anon meeting, I learned that my life would not change unless I took a long look at myself. It was suggested that I get a Sponsor and get busy. My Sponsor suggested I do three things: 1) Attend a meeting at least once a week, same time and same place; 2) Use my Sponsor by sharing things I would not share with anyone else; 3) Follow the Twelve Steps to the best of my ability.

Shortly into my recovery, a fellow member I greatly admired was asked to share at an Al-Anon meeting. He started his story by describing the relationship he had with his children. Then he paused and said, "What I'm talking about is child abuse." He went on to draw an all too familiar picture. It was as if he had watched me and was relating what he had seen. He talked about the children as being little people who laughed and cried and were happy and sad, just like us. He then shared how our wonderful Al-Anon program with its Twelve Steps had given him yet another chance to be a good father. As I listened, I was surrounded by a warm embrace I have felt many times since, and I knew I was not alone. Because of his courage, I also knew there was hope.

Despite the fact that I abused my children in almost every way a father could abuse a child, our program and a loving God has allowed me another opportunity to be a positive member of my family. The relationship I have today with my seven sons and five daughters is the most special in my life. You see, Al-Anon taught me how to love.

TWELVE STEPS

1. We admitted we were powerless over alcohol—that our lives had become unmanageable.
2. Came to believe that a Power greater than ourselves could restore us to sanity.
3. Made a decision to turn our will and our lives over to the care of God *as we understood Him*.
4. Made a searching and fearless moral inventory of ourselves.
5. Admitted to God, to ourselves, and to another human being the exact nature of our wrongs.
6. Were entirely ready to have God remove all these defects of character.
7. Humbly asked Him to remove our shortcomings.
8. Made a list of all persons we had harmed, and became willing to make amends to them all.
9. Made direct amends to such people wherever possible, except when to do so would injure them or others.
10. Continued to take personal inventory and when we were wrong promptly admitted it.
11. Sought through prayer and meditation to improve our conscious contact with God *as we understood Him*, praying only for knowledge of His will for us and the power to carry that out.
12. Having had a spiritual awakening as the result of these steps, we tried to carry this message to others, and to practice these principles in all our affairs.

TWELVE TRADITIONS

1. Our common welfare should come first; personal progress for the greatest number depends upon unity.

2. For our group purpose there is but one authority—a loving God as He may express Himself in our group conscience. Our leaders are but trusted servants—they do not govern.

3. The relatives of alcoholics, when gathered together for mutual aid, may call themselves an Al-Anon Family Group, provided that, as a group, they have no other affiliation. The only requirement for membership is that there be a problem of alcoholism in a relative or friend.

4. Each group should be autonomous, except in matters affecting another group or Al-Anon or AA as whole.

5. Each Al-Anon Family Group has but one purpose: to help families of alcoholics. We do this by practicing the Twelve Steps of AA *ourselves*, by encouraging and understanding our alcoholic relatives, and by welcoming and giving comfort to families of alcoholics.

6. Our Family Groups ought never endorse, finance or lend our name to any outside enterprise, lest problems of money, property and prestige divert us from our primary spiritual aim. Although a separate entity, we should always co-operate with Alcoholics Anonymous.

7. Every group ought to be fully self-supporting, declining outside contributions.

8. Al-Anon Twelfth Step work should remain forever non-professional, but our service centers may employee special workers.

9. Our groups, as such, ought never be organized; but we may create service boards or committees directly responsible to those they serve.

10. The Al-Anon Family Groups have no opinion on outside issues; hence our name ought never be drawn into public controversy.

11. Our public relations policy is based on attraction rather than promotion; we need always maintain personal anonymity at the level of press, radio, films, and TV. We need guard with special care the anonymity of all AA members.

12. Anonymity is the spiritual foundation of all our Traditions, ever reminding us to place principles above personalities.

TWELVE CONCEPTS OF SERVICE

1. The ultimate responsibility and authority for Al-Anon world services belongs to the Al-Anon groups.
2. The Al-Anon Family Groups have delegated complete administrative and operational authority to their Conference and its service arms.
3. The right of decision makes effective leadership possible.
4. Participation is the key to harmony.
5. The rights of appeal and petition protect minorities and insure that they be heard.
6. The Conference acknowledges the primary administrative responsibility of the Trustees.
7. The Trustees have legal rights while the rights of the Conference are traditional.
8. The Board of Trustees delegates full authority for routine management of Al-Anon Headquarters to its executive committees.
9. Good personal leadership at all service levels is a necessity. In the field of world service the Board of Trustees assumes the primary leadership.
10. Service responsibility is balanced by carefully defined service authority and double-headed management is avoided.
11. The World Service Office is composed of selected committees, executives and staff members.
12. The spiritual foundation for Al-Anon's world services is contained in the General Warranties of the Conference, Article 12 of the Charter.

GENERAL WARRANTIES OF THE CONFERENCE

In all proceedings the World Service Conference of Al-Anon shall observe the spirit of the Traditions:

1. that only sufficient operating funds, including an ample reserve, be its prudent financial principle;
2. that no Conference member shall be placed in unqualified authority over other members;
3. that all decisions be reached by discussion vote and whenever possible by unanimity;
4. that no Conference action ever be personally punitive or an incitement to public controversy;
5. that though the Conference serves Al-Anon it shall never perform any act of government; and that like the fellowship of Al-Anon Family Groups which it serves, it shall always remain democratic in thought and action.

INDEX